Grace under pressure

Martial Arts and Sports Hypnosis

Adam Vile, PhD and Jo Biggs

© 2004 by Adam Vile and Jo Biggs. All rights reserved.

All rights reserved. No part of this publication can be reproduced, stored in a retrieval system, or transmitted in any form or by any means, electronic, mechanical, photocopying, recording or otherwise, without the prior permission of the publishers and/or authors.

While every precaution has been taken in the preparation of this book, the publisher assumes no responsibilities for errors or omissions, or for damages resulting from the use of information contained herein.

First published by Lulu Press 2004

In China there was once a man who liked pictures of Dragons, and his furniture and clothing were designed accordingly. His deep affection for dragons was brought to the notice of the dragon god, and one day a real dragon appeared before his window. It is said that he died of fright.

Yamamoto Tsunetomo. <u>Hagakure.</u>

Acknowledgements

There are many people who have made this work possible and it is not possible to thank them all by name. We apologise then that the following list is not complete and for those that we have missed out of the list below we offer heartfelt thanks. You know who you are.

There are giants upon whose shoulders we stand. And we have had many teachers. Richard, Paul, Jamie, Graham, Steve. We thank you, you have put us on the path and given us the means to find our own way to where we are going.

There are friends and loved ones who have supported us, indulged us and helped us more than they can know: Vic, Megan, Richard, Mike, Mum, Dad.

Our greatest joy, our finest teachers, our friends: Zoe, Matt, Taz, Tash.

We thank you all. Your guidance, help and love have been, and continue to be, our guiding light.

Contents

INTRODUCTION 9

CHAPTER 1 - CHALLENGE ME THE TRANCE 15
    JUST CHATTING 15
    FIRST THINGS FIRST 17
    THE ADVENTURE STARTS HERE 18
    OVER THE TOP – GO THERE FIRST. 21
    ONWARDS - BUT FIRST TO SLEEP 26

CHAPTER 2 - PIERCING THE VEIL 29
    WORD SALAD 29
    MAKING FINER AND FINER DISTINCTIONS 32

CHAPTER 3 - SHAKESPEARE DIDN'T HAVE A BIRO. 43
    OF PENS AND SWORDS 43
    MAY WE SUGGEST? 47
    SEE, FEEL, HEAR, RELAX NOW 49

CHAPTER 4 – FINDING YOUR OWN DORIS 53
    THE WAY IN – ENTRANCE 53
    AND IT ALL HAPPENS SO NATURALLY 58
    INTO THE UNKNOWN 61
    SO WHERE IS YOUR DORIS? 63

CHAPTER 5 – KNOWING WHERE YOU ARE HEADING ... 67
    GET SMART, AND THEN SOME 67
    ARE YOU LICKING YOUR LIPS YET? 76

CHAPTER 6 – CHALLENGE YOU THE TRANCE 81
    LET ME TELL YOU HOW 81
    AND NOW YOU CAN RELAX, BIT BY BIT 82

YES,YES,YES…	88
THE COMBINATION METHOD	92
GOING DOWN	94
DOING IT ALL TOGETHER	97
AS I WAS SAYING	98

CHAPTER 7 – WHAT'S DONE IS DONE 101
AND CAN'T BE UNDONE?	101
GETTING TO KNOW YOU	102
ALLOW ME TO INTERVENE	105
IMAGINE THIS	108

CHAPTER 8 - JOINING UP THE DOTS 113
UP TO THE THRESHOLD	113
EXCUSE US FOR BEING FORMAL	114
DOING IT FOR YOURSELF	117
AND FINALLY…	119

CHAPTER 9 – THERE BE DRAGONS 121
DO THEY BREATHE FIRE?	121
CHEN AND YANG	127

APPENDIX – THE WIZARDS SPELL BOOK 133
MOTIVATION	133
RELAXATION	136
PERSONAL POWER	137
ENERGY	140

APPENDIX - DISTINCTIONS 144
SUBMODALITY DISTINCTIONS	144
CONSCIOUS - UNCONSCIOUS MINDS	144

BIBLIOGRAPHY 145
INDEX 147

Introduction

> *I once knew a little boy in England who asked his father "Do fathers always know more than their sons?" and the father said "Yes". The next question was "Daddy, who invented the steam engine?" and the father said "James Watt". Then the son came back with " – but why didn't James Watt's father invent it?"*
>
> Gregory Bateson, <u>How much do you know?</u>

Miyamoto Mushashi, a 16th century Samurai suffered his only defeat at the hands of Muso Gonnosuke, an expert with the 4' staff. This was not the first time that the two had met in combat. Years earlier they had fought their first duel. That time Miyamoto had won and had spared Muso's life, he said, in order that Muso could meditate on his defeat. Muso did meditate, on a mountain (which seems mandatory in these circumstances) for between two and ten years, at which point he had a divine insight about how to defeat Mushasi, this master of the two swords, by using a short staff. He descended the mountain found, challenged and defeated Mushashi, and in respect allowed him to live. Muso went on to form a school and teach his skills. Though it had evidently been invaluable to him, he did not require that his students meditate for ten years on a mountain in order to learn these skills.

We remember back in the 1980's when there was a series of advertisements in a national martial arts magazine, which offered prospective students a black belt in a month. We also remember the story of a television reporter who managed to go from no grade to black-belt in a single days training. Now, we accept the ideas of accelerated learning, in fact we know that you certainly can step up learning at quite a rate. Much of our own work is focussed around helping martial artists and athletes to learn and improve skills at a vastly accelerated rate. But we do wonder just how comparable a one-day and a three-year black belt is?

On the flip side of this we also know of teachers who teach one skill at a time, in the order in which they learnt it, in the way in which they learnt it, for a predetermined length of time. It always takes a painfully long time to achieve anything. Yet the final quality of that achievement is high and well deserved. There is of course some middle ground.

Some skills take years to develop, and little time to learn. In this book we offer you the distillation of our own meditation and analysis of the structure of the skills that we have taken years to assimilate, learn and develop. We have learnt from great teachers and we have learnt from terrible teachers. We have learnt from our students, we have learnt from our peers and we have learnt from each other. We keep on learning, and we always will. We have read many books, observed many experts, but most of all we have tried things, and done things and learnt from getting it wrong and right.

This book is a book, not just for you to read, but for you to engage with. It is meant to be experienced. Some of it may seem unusual at first, and perhaps second and third, reading but we assure you every word is carefully crafted and thought about, and every story, paragraph and activity is designed to build a whole experience that is both meaningful and instructional. After the first reading, feel free to dip in at appropriate places, and you may find Chapter 8 a useful summary.

Introduction

There is everything you need in these pages to begin the process of developing exquisite skills as a hypnotist, teacher, sportsman, martial artist and coach. Of course in a little over one hundred pages it is hard to provide completeness, and so we have focussed specifically on developing those skills that we know work, and that we have used successfully in our own work. In particular, skills that specifically relate to martial arts and sports, performance and coaching.

Chapter 1 introduces the idea of leading and pacing, and begins with the "power circle" to look at the powerful idea of anchoring. Chapter 2 is an appeal to those of you who find the terminology of psychology, linguistics and hypnosis hard to get underneath, to persevere. It also deals with the way in which we represent ideas in our minds and in our language. Chapter 3 focuses on the writing of suggestions and shows how to write a powerful relaxation script. Chapter 4 explores strategies for success, and leads directly to Chapter 5 where ways of making goals and objectives that are compelling are discussed.

Chapter 6 is where we examine hypnosis in depth, and where we introduce a number of ways of inducing trance. Chapter 7 looks at the utilisation of those trance states and Chapter 8 pulls this altogether giving a suggested framework for ways of working with groups and individuals. Chapter 9 offers some words of advice that we hope you find valuable. In the appendix you will find a number of scripts for you to use in your own contexts.

This book has its frame of reference in martial arts, but it is equally appropriate in any sporting context. The skills required of a martial artists - speed, power, flexibility, motivation, relaxation, clearness of thought, energy, accuracy, and many more; are just as important in all sports from sailing, through athletics to chess, albeit to differing degrees. And it doesn't have to stop inside a sporting context, these skills, and others that you will learn as you engage with this book, are just as valuable in your family and at work, for your friends and loved ones, and of course yourself. Coaches, athletes, teachers, martial artists, competitors and practitioners will all find, in this book, things of value.

A word to the wise; realise your limitations. Yet whilst working at the boundaries of your knowledge and ability, continue to strive to overcome them, until you find new ones, at a higher level. The book is not the learning. The book is not the knowledge. Feedback is essential in any kind of learning, so make sure that you listen and observe. Ask advice and listen to it. This way you will always find teachers, everywhere.

Our challenge to you then is to take part in the pages of this book, do the activities, think through and about and over and underneath the ideas, use them in your training, teaching, coaching and daily life, follow up on the background reading, seek out teachers and experts, learn and then take everything you know and come back and teach us something. Enjoy the book.

Chapter 1 - Challenge me the Trance

> *A monk once asked Joshu "I have just arrived at the monastery and don't know the proper way to go about practice, please tell me what to do." Joshu said "Have you eaten breakfast?" The monk replied "Yes, I have just finished eating" Joshu said "then wash your bowl"*
> Sekkei Harada, <u>The Essence of Zen</u>.

JUST CHATTING

It was late, past midnight, and tomorrow would be an early start. Two martial artists were sat at the kitchen table, drinking coffee and chatting. In the morning, which was by now just a few hours away, they would be teaching on a national course. It wasn't unusual though for them to be up so late, as they rarely saw each other and were only really able to catch up at times like this. Quite often the conversation centred around the qualities of various martial arts, and on new techniques that had been learned or developed. However this night their minds were on the forthcoming course, and the focus of this particular discussion was training, learning, technique, performance and skill. Questions were asked such as: How can we teach better? How can the students become more skilful? How can they learn more quickly? How can they develop an appropriate understanding of the underlying principles of their art? What can we do, as experienced teachers, to make the difference that makes the difference? And most importantly, what can we do *tomorrow* to begin to start the process?

Time was getting on, and morning was approaching. The coffee was running out. One of the pair steered the chat towards Hypnosis as a possible direction, after all it had been seen to be very valuable in accelerated learning and sports performance enhancement (Ligget, 2000). Ever the sceptic, the other dismissed Hypnosis and began to explain in great detail just how, although valuable, it wouldn't work for everyone, and certainly not on him. He wasn't really very convinced of any benefits - maybe in some cases, but certainly not in groups or in a team, group or class situation. And besides, it was time to get some sleep.

Before retiring to bed, they spoke about Hypnosis some more, throwing around ideas and questions. It was agreed that, being an open-minded sort of chap, the sceptic would allow his friend to have a go and "fail" in hypnotising him. At the very most perhaps he could succeed in allowing him to relax deeply and shut his eyes (after all they both could do with a rest). While his eyes were closed, and he was relaxed, his friend talked to him softly, inducing a deeply hypnotic state.

When he opened his eyes, after 45 minutes, he was alert and awake, and said how he felt energised by the experience, which was very interesting indeed. It was particularly amazing because of the brief time that he had had his eyes closed. His friend pointed out the time to him and said that he had actually been chatting to him non-stop for 45 minutes!! The sceptic looked at his friend and said "Curious, I'll have to look into this" Now maybe you think that it is not difficult to talk non-stop for 45 minutes, you probably know people who do this all of the time. But do they take you into a relaxing state and bring you back energised and awake? Could you do this, to others? to yourself? Wouldn't this be a useful and valuable skill?

Of course, there wasn't much sleeping done that night, and the next morning the training was lead by two extremely enthusiastic teachers. That was 10 years ago, and over that time the "looking-into" became much more than that. Now that sceptic and his friend are the co-authors of this book. A book that pulls together their experiences over all of those years, of developing learning, exploring and (most importantly) **doing-it**.

FIRST THINGS FIRST

This book is not a heavy academic tome, rather it is a practical guide, in the form of a conversation with you, the reader. You will learn, you will explore, you will discover and hopefully you will be entertained. Throughout out this book we will stop and tell you little stories, big stories and give you things to do. Everything in this book is important; nothing is there just to fill up space. We are going to give you many things in this book - ideas, advice knowledge, experiences. But if we could give you just one thing, it would be this simple piece of advice – don't just read it, don't just think about it, **do it.**

This is so important, because we want you to have an experience and to develop an understanding of how to utilize basic hypnotic techniques to improve your martial arts. We want to help you build beliefs that will empower and help you to **do it** better, faster and to enjoy it even more. You know especially, as a martial artist or sports person, that time spent on the mat, on the track, in the gym, on target or in the dojo *doing-it* is the most important time in your training and learning. And in the end you stand or fall by your ability to do-it yourself, and to teach others to do-it. You may like to get a journal or notebook to use as you go through this book, as some of the things that we will ask you to do will involve writing, and you may like to note ideas and anything else that surprises you.

THE ADVENTURE STARTS HERE

> **Telling a story: Do-it**
>
> Go back and think of something that you learned to do really well. For example learning to punch, perhaps a specific punch, or a kick. You can choose any physical technique you like, but it must be one that you have learnt to do extremely well.
>
> Now you have 5 minutes to tell a story about how that learning. Either imagine that you are telling the story to someone, or actually do-it, tell that story to someone. You have 5 minutes; so make sure that you fill it. Use the whole 5 minutes.
>
> Perhaps you could write this story down (do-it). We will come back to it later.

So let's go on the adventure right now, and let's begin as we mean to go on, let's do-it.

There is of course no sense in not starting right at the very beginning, and so we would like to start by asking you to consider one thing very carefully, one thing that will help you to make a difference, not just in the Martial arts teaching and training, but everywhere in your life. There is one tool that is invaluable to us, it helps us communicate, and share feelings and emotions. That tool is none other than - voice. And here is our first trick, our first tip for you. It relates to the voice and of course it really needs to be shown face to face or heard. However by doing the following exercise you can begin to develop the correct technique to gain control not only of what you say, but how you say it.

> **Voice Control: Do-it**
>
> First of all take the first and index fingers from your right hand and place them on your nose. Now say "*This is my nose*"
>
> Now breathe out and place the fingers on your mouth: say "*this is my mouth*"
>
> Repeat this process for your chest and stomach. Each time lowering your voice to make it sound more relaxing and calm.
>
> Now make your voice sound *curious about relaxing*. Now make it sound intrigued. And finally, confident.

So the difference between a relaxing, calm, guiding voice and an annoying, irritating grating voice is that one is nasal and the other starts from deep down in the stomach. Imagine what it would be like for a child to be read a bedtime story in a whiney, nasal voice. We are pretty confident that our children would not find that a suitable preparation for getting ready to go to sleep!! What about a nasal salesman? Would you buy your goods form someone with a voice like a strimmer? (Maybe if you were buying a strimmer I suppose.) Now let's see just how relaxing you can sound. Did you write your story down? (Have we started to do it yet?).

> **Voice Exercise 2: Do-It**
>
> Now read your story with a different tone of voice. One that is relaxed and comes from the stomach as opposed to one that comes through your nose.

Are you starting to sound different yet? Good, we hope you are. You see it is so important, when you say words like *learn*, that you say them in a way that encourages learning. You must be confident, and say words meaningfully and with enthusiasm. Now don't get us wrong, we are not suggesting over the top enthusiasm, try and do-it with gentle enthusiasm. With learning,

Grace Under Pressure

for example, we want you to be able to recreate a positive, curious, feeling and experience for your students, and you can start to do that by correct use of your voice.

We know that you already teach people to punch , kick, run, hit, slice, pass or grapple well, whatever your speciality. But there is more to teaching than demonstrating, and there is more to learning than copying (although these are very important parts of the learning puzzle), and there is more to sports and martial arts expertise and success than pure physical technique. Right now we would like you to consider this very important additional piece of the puzzle. And it concerns your ability to know what you are aiming at. If, for example, you are going to ask someone to really enjoy relaxing, what is that going to feel like? What is it going to sound like? And what is it going to look like? So here we go again, time for you to do it.

Relax: Do-It

For this do-it you will need access to a video camera, perhaps you can borrow one if you don't already have one. Now put in the corner of the room, sit yourself down in front of it and relax, and enjoy. Do this for ten minutes, you could even shut your eyes, and allow your mind to go away on a journey of its own.

Now watch the tape. What do you see? Does your breathing change, does your skin colour change? When you were relaxing what did you feel (write this down – do it). Good.

Record it: Do-it
Now tape record yourself reading your story. Listen to it. How do you sound?

It is a good idea for you to ask someone else's opinion on your voice tone and control. Pick someone you trust and play the tape to them, then listen very carefully to what they say. If you are doing something that isn't working, **do something else.** But beware, because here is another piece of the puzzle: *people have very different experiences and respond in very different ways.* For example, a quiet walk in the park might be relaxing to you, but may bring back terrifying memories for someone else. Perhaps now you are beginning to see what makes **do-it** such a beneficial experience?

OVER THE TOP – GO THERE FIRST.

A story is told of Kusonogi Masashige, a Samurai of great martial prowess and loyalty, who held off a great army with a handful of men at Chihaya fortress on mount Kongo. His men were inspired by his martial ability, his tactics and by his tenacious resolve. It is a quality of good leadership to never ask anyone to do anything that you wouldn't do yourself. For example, during the First World War, the junior officers charged towards the enemy's trenches with their men, at the front. If you wish to help people to relax, in order that they can begin to make the changes and improvements that they need to make, you will need to be able to relax yourself. Everything that they experience you must have already experienced. And so the process is more about taking the lead, going to the destination yourself first and encouraging them to follow. This is why it is imperative that you do-it. *First.*

The next do-it, is a variation of a technique that was first demonstrated to us by a therapist and martial artist, Garner

Thomson. He called it the *power circle*, and it is a mixture of visualisation and anchoring. We will explain these terms after you have completed the exercise.

> **The Power Circle: Do-it**
>
> Stand up, and imagine a circle on the ground with you at the centre. This circle should be sized so that if you were to step forwards you would be stepping out of the circle. Can you see it? What colour is it?
>
> Now stand with your feet together in the centre of the circle, and imagine yourself calm and relaxed. Take yourself back to a time when you were particularly calm and relaxed. See what you saw then, hear what you heard, and feel what you felt at your most relaxed. This is the *centre*.
>
> Now step forwards into stance (as you do raise your hands in an 'on guard' position), outside of the circle, and imagine yourself confident and powerful. Take yourself back to a time when you felt that confident, that powerful. See what you saw then, hear what you heard, and feel what you felt. Notice the sensations on your body. This is *to the outside*.
>
> Now step back, and as you do recall those centre feelings, feelings of relaxation and calmness. Intensify those feelings as you step. Now step forwards, into stance, and as you do recall those sensations of being *outside*, confident, powerful, fast. Take those feelings and double them, intensify them.
>
> Now continue to step backwards and forwards, constantly changing your state from calm and *centred*, to powerfully, confidently *outside* the circle. Every time you do this double the intensity of the feelings. How do you feel now?

Weigh Anchor

We want you to feel good every time you step forward or backward. You need to have the sensation of you stepping being your anchor. This concept, the concept of *anchor*, first elaborated in the work of Grinder and Bandler (1977) but known to hypnotists for many years before, comes from an application of the work of Pavlov around the turn of the century. He was a Russian scientist from the behaviourist school who demonstrated the power of stimulus-response theory by conditioning dogs to respond *as if* they were about to be fed, when they heard a bell ring. He did this by ringing the bell just before he fed them. Dogs salivate when they think of food, and eventually when Pavlov rang the bell and didn't deliver food, the dogs still salivated. There are many times and places where we as humans respond in the same way to specific stimulus. For example, isn't there a particular song (normally known as *our-song* by couples!!) which triggers particular memories and thoughts? Or doesn't the sight of a particular person fill you with dread? A very severe case of anchoring is a phobia, in which the very sight of the tiniest spider can make an otherwise fearless person run and scream. And if we don't think that we are as unsophisticated as Pavlov's hungry canines, how many of us remember all too vividly the school bell!!

Anchors are relatively straightforward to create and can be in any form - a word, a picture, a sound, a movement. They have to be unique for each state that you want to access and they have to be a single item. In the case of phobias you only have to see the stimulus (spider) one time and respond (run and scream) in the way you did on that first occurrence, to generate a strong anchor for any time you see a spider in the future.

The phobia anchor is an example of a negative anchor, but the most valuable use is in generating positive states. Anchors are fantastically powerful, allowing you to access previous positive and powerful states instantaneously. If you have done the power circle do-it then you have already installed anchors for confident–

powerful and calm-relaxed, just by stepping forwards and backwards.

Another aspect of this power circle was the *on guard*. The movement of your hands rising upwards was the anchor to fire off speed and power and confidence. I am sure that you can see that this would be particularly valuable in any competitive fighting art, for example kickboxing. Now go back and do this exercise again and get good at it, good at generating the different states and creating the anchors. We want you to begin the discipline of noticing, and in the case of this exercise particularly focus on noticing the very different states that occur **before**, **during** and **after** you make each move and fire off the anchor.

Anchoring: Do-it

Decide on a resourceful state that would be of use to you. Confidence, calmness, serenity, happiness…

Decide on an anchor. Something simple. Perhaps touching your thumb and forefinger together?

Now close your eyes and imagine a time when you felt most perfectly in this state. See what you saw while in that state, feel what you felt and hear what you heard. Now take those feelings and intensify them, double the intensity and double it again until it is almost as intense as it can be.

Now fire the anchor (touch your thumb and finger together) and allow the intensity to increase just that bit more.

Repeat three times. Clearing the memory each time. Perhaps, in between, thinking of something else.

Now open your eyes, wipe the resourceful memory clean, look around. Now fire the anchor. How do you feel? Curious isn't it?

Eye See

You can see things in two different ways. Things out there, and things inside. When you see something that you generate from the inside, like for example the imaginary power circle, then you are *visualising*. Visualisations can be projected outside (like the circle) or can remain inside, for example when running through a movie of a memory of, say, the perfect execution of a technique, movement or form. Some people appear to believe that they have difficulty visualising, but most of us have had the experience of buying something, for example curtains or a TV, and having to imagine what it would be like when we get it home and put it in the living room. Some of us can even buy shirts without trying them on, being pretty sure what they will look like when they are matched with those blue trousers.

If you think you aren't good at visualisation the next do-it is for you. Do do-it, because visualisation is such an important skill. It is central to much of sports psychology even though some authors believe that it is overrated (Edgette and Rowen, 2003) and it is essential in the generation of states, both remembered and created. In chapter 2 we will explore visualisation and state creation in depth and in chapter 7 we will look at powerful ways of using visualisation to improve muscle memory.

Visualisation: Do-it

Practice your visualisation skills in the following way:

Pick your favourite mug or cup. Look at it intently. Now close your eyes and picture it in your mind. Describe it. Open your eyes and check to see if you got it right. Notice every curve and join, notice the colour variations, and proportions. Close your eyes again and see if this time you can see more. Continue until you have a perfect internal image.

> (…)
> Now imagine it purple and yellow with green spots and a picture of an orange unicorn on it. (If your original mug was like that, then where on earth did you buy it?!)

ONWARDS - BUT FIRST TO SLEEP

We hope that you have done everything that we have asked you to do in this chapter. If you have then you will have noticed some important things, and you will have noticed the difference. Now when you start to do group work you will be able to tell when people are doing each exercise properly. If you continue to practice the exercises and follow our suggestions here and throughout the rest of this book you will start to build your skill set in order that you can use sports hypnosis to learn more efficiently and build beliefs in yourself and others. We all know the importance of building and having strong belief. Without belief that he could break the 4-minute mile barrier, Roger Bannister would not have even tried. Everyone said it couldn't be done. But it was, and now is no longer a barrier for any professional mile runner. That which was once held back by beliefs, is now achievable because of more powerful beliefs.

So far in this chapter we have looked at some of the skills that form the building blocks of successful sports hypnosis and already we are starting to develop and refine them. Throughout this book you will have opportunities to continue to refine and develop them even more. Already we have ability to change state quickly and anchor it, and we have the ability to use our voice productively. This is such an important skill because if we are going to improve people's abilities and change targets with hypnosis then our voice is a key tool. We want vocals that make people sparkle.

Before we start the next chapter we would like you to take time to integrate and assimilate the learnings of this chapter. Quite literally we want you to *sleep on it*. We would like you to lie down and put on some gentle music to fall asleep to or not, however you prefer. And do the final do-it;

Integration: Do-it
Lying comfortably with some relaxing music in the background begin to relax. Relax. You are going to relax all the muscles in your body, from the top of your head to the tip of your toes. Start now, take it slowly, noticing each muscle as it becomes loose and comfortable.
When you get to your feet think of a time in the next few weeks when you will need some confidence. When will that be? What will you be doing? Make a movie of this in your head; make sure that the movie is at the beginning, and that you can see yourself on the screen. Now access the power circle, those feelings of confidence and power, and when you feel as confident in yourself as you need to be, step into the movie (actually see yourself become part of the move) and then (only then, when you are feeling as confident as you can) run the movie forwards. Talk to yourself, in a positive and confident and positive way as you run through the movie.
Do this a few times, and in as many future scenarios as you want.

At the end of this chapter our aim is that you feel confident and are able to walk powerfully. Of course you have to walk before you run, and so in the next chapter we will be running. Sleep well.

Chapter 2 - Piercing the veil

> *"Would you please tell me which way I ought to go from here"*
> *"That depends a good deal on where you want to get to," said the cat.*
> *"I don't much care where-" said Alice.*
> *"Then it doesn't much matter which way you go," said the cat.*
> *"- so long as I get somewhere," Alice added by way of an explanation.*
> *"Oh you are sure to do that," said the cat, "as long as you walk long enough."*
> Lewis Caroll, <u>Alice in Wonderland</u>.

WORD SALAD

Recently I walked the 4-day Inca trail to Macchu Picchu in Peru. It is a beautiful walk through the Andes, passing mountainous terrain and high altitude jungle. The views are spectacular, and the effort to climb to the highest point worth it. At one point, the tour guide offered us a choice, to follow the normal tourist path, or to take another, higher, less trodden path. We chose the latter, but I couldn't help wondering what we were missing. But then wouldn't that have been the same whichever we had taken? Arriving at the sun gate just in time to see the sun rise over this exquisite monument I could understand what it was that drove the Incas to build such a powerful edifice perched on the side of a mountain. Nonetheless I was a little disappointed that my journey was coming to an end. The purpose of my journey was never *just* to arrive at Macchu Picchu.

Grace Under Pressure

Well, did you sleep on it? We hope you did. There are some people who will, when they buy a book, flick through or rush straight to the end (without passing GO, without collecting £200), perhaps looking for the *big secret*. There are also those who read the end of the story in the final chapter first, to find out what happens. But what makes them think that everything of importance is at the end? We have news for you; the big secret is not at the end of this book. *It is all of the way through it.* If there is one thing that we would like you to learn, it is this: it is in the doing, in the application, practice, performance and perfection of the exercises you find in this book that the secrets will be revealed to you. And now we have just given the secret away!!

I am reminded of a particular young man, a number of years ago, who persistently would ask me for explanations of words. Now its not that I was particularly verbose, or even sesquipedalian[1], but sometimes the only way to elegantly and economically express a concept is by using words that encapsulate ideas succinctly. Now I do believe very strongly that it is important, when building rapport, to ensure that you are able to communicate in such a way that your ideas and meanings are shared, so that everyone involved in the communication makes the same meanings. And this is something that we should strive for. But the responsibility for communication lies with each of us. It is not that anyone would use long words for the sake of it, but there is a place when they are used as terms of reference. Terms of reference are just that, they are chosen specifically in a certain context as anchors,

---

[1] Sesquipedalian – this word comes from the Latin meaning "Six feet Long" and is used (usually by people who are sesquipedalian) to describe those who like to use long words!! It is a totally unnecessary word, but it is nonetheless very cool.

Piercing The Veil

to help us re-access a whole gamut of supporting ideas and theories.

Like many of his (our) generation this young man had muddled through school, driven down by other people's low expectations. His non-achievement was accepted, not challenged, and responsibility was shifted away from problems in teaching to his perceived problems with learning: he was quickly labelled dyslexic. His spelling and handwriting were atrocious and many a time he would ask me for a definition of a word or ask how something was spelled.

One weekend we were due to be teaching a group of around 120 students. In the planning of the event we were discussing learning and teaching, and there was a constant stream of words being used in the context of this discussion that seemed to require explanation. I asked Jo why he thought it was that his vocabulary seemed so limited. He told me that he had not been very good at school (but that he had shone in other areas) and that one particular memory that he had was of a teacher throwing a blackboard rubber at him when he made a mistake. This is something that I think many of us may remember, but perhaps not as such a vivid and defining memory.

That night I popped out and went to a late night shop on the Fulham Road and bought quite a hefty dictionary and thesaurus for a couple of pounds. The next day, while he was teaching, I took this book, and went and watched. At one point, a student asked him a question, and he called over to me to help him understand the meaning of some of the terms. I stood up, walked nearer, and threw the book at him; it caught him on the side of the head. Fortunately Jo did take this well, and everyone found it funny. I told him to look the word up, and then (and only then) when he had made the effort to do that, if he still had some questions or required further explanation, he could come and discuss them with me.

Around two months later, I bought a martial arts magazine to pass the time whilst waiting for a train, and as I was flicking through, I noticed an article, which interested me. I read it and was about to turn the page when suddenly my attention was drawn to the name of the author. It was that same young man who had had such low expectations and had failed to catch the dictionary and thesaurus (combined) with the side of his head. And what's more, the article was well written, well informed, and liberally splattered with the sort of words that previously I would have had to explain. Now, if you haven't guessed yet, this young man is a co-author of this book. He has become an expert in hypnotic communication and the associated linguistics.

MAKING FINER AND FINER DISTINCTIONS

Enough chatting now, it will soon be time for your next do-it. But first, there are a number of terms and ideas that we need to get across. What is important now is that you begin to develop your skills in visualisation, and in particular in noticing elements of our visualisations at finer and finer levels of granularity. We are going to be exploring very fine distinctions known as **modalities**. The first in-depth exploration of these ideas can be found in the work of Bandler and Grinder (1977) and Bandler (1982), who define them both pragmatically and technically. This is not an issue as you already have all of the resources to accessing the meanings in the language of modalities and sub-modalities. Don't you? Before we explore the details, here is a valuable do-it.

Piercing The Veil

> **Noticing Distinctions: Do-it**
>
> How do you represent sporting success inside yourself?
>
> Think back to a memory of one of your finest moments in your martial arts history, a time when you shone, when your technique was as good as it could be, when you were extremely successful. Now pay attention to your representation. Notice what you see, notice what you hear, notice what you smell, taste, feel. Write it down.
>
> Intensify the feelings. And anchor them. Choose an anchor that is appropriate to you. Call this anchor X.

Our primary modalities of taste, smell, touch, sight and hearing (not necessarily in this order), allow us to attach meaning to any experience real or imaginary, remembered or constructed. They also allow us to make comparisons between representations. Before you do this do-it, please make sure that you have done the previous one and have anchor X installed.

> **Noticing Distinctions 2: Do-it**
>
> How do you represent sporting failure?
>
> Think back to a memory of one of your worst moments in your Martial Arts or Sporting history, a time when you stunk, when your technique was awful when you were terrible. Now pay attention again to your representation. Notice what you see, notice what you hear, notice what you smell, taste, feel. Write it down.
>
> Intensify the feelings. And anchor them. Choose an anchor that is appropriate to you. Call this anchor Y.
>
> Fire the X anchor from the previous do-it (we don't want you feeling bad for too long!!).
>
> Now compare your representations of X and Y. How do you represent failure, success?

What did you notice, what was the same in these representation, what was different? It is clear that we make representations of internal experiences in many different ways, and in ways that make sense to us. This perceptual organisation of experience refines and makes distinctions between internal resources. The value in knowing how things are represented and related is that resources (like confidence, power, concentration etc.) can be immediately accessed just by recalling the structure of that experience. Even more useful and explicit distinctions can be made, known as **sub-modalities**. These break down each of the internal representations into significant sub-distinctions. For example when you look at your image of X is it colour or black and white, is it fuzzy or clear. In the film *Dead Poets Society*, Robin Williams plays an eccentric teacher who in one scene asks his pupils to climb on the desks in the classroom so that they can get a different perspective, he could have discussed the idea with them, but by asking the students to actively engage in the process he allowed them to access a whole new experience. And now it is time for *you* to fully engage in an experience.

Our primary modalities match directly our senses - taste (Gustatory), smell (Olfactory), touch (Kinaesthetic), sight (Visual), and hearing (Auditory) - and allow us to attach meaning to any experience and make comparisons between different representations. It may sound strange, but you may see that once you experience this for yourself, by noticing finer and finer distinctions you begin to get a feeling for how you organise your own internal experiences. This is a valid model of the way that we make sense of the world; it allows us to think about how to alter the structure of our experiences by altering the structure of our representations, you will see (feel, hear, experience) how this works in the next do-it.

> **Finer Distinctions: Do-it**
>
> Access X again. Pay attention to the visual aspect of the structure. Notice the following distinctions. Is it:
>
> Fuzzy – focussed;
>
> Black and white – Coloured;
>
> A movie – A still picture;
>
> Panoramic – Bordered?
>
> What other distinctions can you see that perhaps are not on this list?
>
> Notice also whether you are in the picture and you can see yourself (*disassociated*) or if you are looking at the picture through your own eyes (*associated*)
>
> What other distinctions can you notice?
>
> Now change these aspects of your representation of X one by one, notice the difference. For example, if you make the picture black and white (if it was coloured) does that intensify or reduce the power of the experience?
>
> Particularly play with the idea of being associated and then disassociated. Notice the distinctions.

As you can see we have divided the visual aspect of your experience into a number of sub distinctions - for example between black and white and coloured. These distinctions are known as sub-modalities, and it is these sub-modalities that allow us to make exquisitely fine changes, in just the right place to make the difference that makes the difference.

Let's give a simple and direct example of this. A runner may be attempting to improve power, confidence and self-belief by visualising herself winning the race. She sees herself crossing the line, and being in front. But how much more of a valid experience do you think that she would have if she were to hear the crowd cheering? and how specifically was their cheering, was it quiet? Was the sound rich, loud, echoing, vibrating? Was there harmony, rhythm? What was the pitch, pace, timbre? Where was the sound coming from? Can you feel it yet? These distinctions are the main auditory distinctions.

> **Making a list : Do-it**
>
> This do-it is simple. Go back through the text, go inside and make a representation of anything (pick something pleasant!!), think and write. Write down all of the sub-modality distinctions that you can think of in the three main systems: visual, auditory, and kinaesthetic. **Do** do-it, because you will need them later. We have started the table for you below (and you will find a more comprehensive table in the appendix)

Visual	Auditory	Kinaesthetic
Fuzzy-Focussed	Loud-Quiet	Warm - Cold
		Light - Heavy

And now it is time for you to practice with these sub-modalities.

> **The really powerful power circle: Do-it**
>
> Go back to the power circle from the previous chapter, and repeat it. But this time we would like you to add finer and finer sub-modality distinctions to your representations, and modify them to give you the best, most exquisite feelings associated with your anchors.
>
> First re-run the power circle. And as you recall a time that was particularly relaxed, change the sub-modalities in all systems, until you find yourself the most relaxed ever.
>
> Now do the same with the power and confidence representation. It is so important to see what you saw, hear what you heard and feel what you felt, but you may also like to smell what you smelled and taste what you tasted if that is appropriate.
>
> *(Continued..)*

Piercing The Veil

> Use all of the sub-modality distinctions to make your representations exquisite. And *now* add a soundtrack.
>
> As you go forwards and backwards, building up the feelings of power, confidence and relaxation alternately, move with the most motivating and powerful soundtrack you know playing constantly. Just at the right pitch and timbre, volume....Turn up the bass....You know.
>
> And how does that make you feel?

Did you have fun? Did you notice the changes? Now maybe it is time to go and get a dictionary.

Now it may seem that so far we haven't even mentioned hypnosis yet - don't worry, we will. But all of this is preparation, laying the groundwork so that when you do come to the bit about Hypnotising someone, you have all of the resources that you need to achieve whatever it is that they want to achieve. By giving you one piece at a time, and allowing you time to integrate each piece into a whole, we are setting you up for success. You are setting yourself up for success. Now, the following exercise may seem familiar, it was taught by Paul McKenna. This is a basic but effective method of improving performance, and it was taught on a course, primarily for atheletes.

> **Athletic performance: Do-it**
>
> Whatever sport you have chosen as the one in which you want to succeed, watch an example of the very highest-level performance that you can.
>
> Now relax and slow your breathing down.
>
> Make a picture of this sport being performed at this level.
>
> Clear the picture and then make the picture again, this time with one major difference: it is now you performing the sport. Build up your performance using the same modalities and submodalities as the original performance.

> (...)
>
> Make it rich and compelling. Enhance the feelings, images, and sounds as you experience yourself performing at this wonderfully superior level.
>
> Now relax, and look into the future. Using all of the modalities and sub-modalities, see, hear, feel yourself performing at this level in the future.
>
> Now choose a specific date and time in the future to perform really well, and experience yourself doing so.

As you have probably already discovered, this is a particularly powerful exercise, and can be used to make profound changes. As we mentioned earlier there are secrets in each and every chapter.

Now it is time for you to combine all of the exercises in the first chapter together, and integrate and consolidate your learning so far. In particular you would benefit from practicing your vocal skills and your skills in facilitating relaxation and noticing when you have achieved relaxation in others. The best way to do this is to find a willing partner and talk them through this exercise you have just completed, as you talk to them you should pay attention to the physical changes in them. The colour of their face, the depth of their breathing, their shoulders rising and falling, their eyes... Pay particular attention to the way in which these changes occur as you alter their modalities and sub-modalities.

The following excerpt is from a transcript of a session run by Adam with a Martial Artist who is having difficulty motivating himself to train. This session is a transcript of an actual session, and it can be seen in a forthcoming training video. It is an example of how a session may proceed. Of course, you will put

Piercing The Veil

your own ideas and personality into every session that you run, but at this stage you may like to use this transcript as a guide.

Adam: *Ok, Rick, so you want to have more motivation to train?*

Rick: *Yeah, I know I should, but I can't... you know, and with my black-belt grading coming up...I dunno.*

Adam: *When is your next training session?*

Rick: *Tomorrow.*

Adam: *Ok so would you like to sit comfortably now and allow yourself to relax, and as you do so would you allow yourself to breathe a little more slowly now... and as you do that you could start to see your self training* (Adam's voice changes in pitch and tempo so that when he says relax, it really does sound relaxing. Rick's eyes close and as he physically relaxes his shoulders drop, letting loose all tensions).

Adam: *And now that you are beginning to relax, and I don't know just how relaxed you can become, I want to draw your attention inside, and to a time that you were particularly motivated....to do something...Anything. It doesn't matter what it was, as long as you were extremely motivated. Do you have that?*

Rick: *Yes*

Adam: *That's right, you do.* (There are noticeable physical changes in Rick's face and body, his breathing speeds up a little and his face reddens. He smiles). *Good, and while you are there, see what you saw, hear what you heard and feel what you feel. And now Rick I want you to notice very clear distinctions. First in the visual field, is the image in colour or in black and white? Moving or still? Panoramic or bordered?*

Rick (Slowly). *Colour...Still...Border.*

Adam: *Good. And are you in the picture or are you looking through your eyes?*

Rick: *Looking.*

Adam: *Excellent. And now, (don't tell me) what is it that you can hear? Are the sounds loud or soft? Shrill or deep? Far away or nearby? Is their music? What music?*

Rick: *Deep... Music... A beat... Loud... Near.*

Adam: *And how does that make you feel? Warm perhaps? Is there pressure? Light or heavy? Vibrations?*

Rick: *Just warm..*

Adam: *Ok so, Warm, Colour, Still, Bordered, That Music, Loud. Now Rick I would like you to imagine yourself training tomorrow. Make a picture of yourself training, but make sure that you are not looking at yourself, but looking as if through your own eyes. And see what you can see, hear what you can hear and feel what you can feel. Make the picture in colour, put a border around it. Great. (Rick clearly is becoming more animated, he is flushing in the face again, and his breathing rate is increasing). Now add that music to your picture, can you hear it? No... turn it up. That's right. And can you feel that warm feeling that you get when you are totally motivated?*

Rick: *(looking as if he is ready to go and train right now!!) Yes.*

Adam: *And let's call that motivation Rick's Motivation-X. And I want you to take that Motivation-X and add it to another training session the day after tomorrow. Have you done it yet? There are always tomorrows to every tomorrow, take that Motivation-X and apply it to the training session after tomorrows tomorrow... and all of the tomorrows....Now how do you feel?*

Rick: *Great.*

Adam: *And now, when you think about training, how do you feel?*

Rick: *(goes inside and checks). Great. I think that I am going to really enjoy training tomorrow.*

Adam: *And the day after tomorrow?*

Rick: *Yes.*

Adam: *Motivation-X, remember.*

Rick *(Smiles, and begins to flush). Yes... Can we try something else? That was great.*

And now it is time for this chapter to end, and the next one to start. Now that we have finished the washing up that is. I am sure that you can guess what your homework is. That's right, go out and buy that dictionary, learn the terms and start, but never stop, making those distinctions.

Chapter 3 - Shakespeare didn't have a biro.

> "Of Shakespeare's mind and manners brightly shines,
> In his well turned and true filled lines,
> In each of which he seems to shake a lance,
> To brandish at the eyes of ignorance"
>
> Ben Johnson

OF PENS AND SWORDS

You have already learnt a great deal, and there is so much more still to go. On the way there have already been lots of long words to learn, understand, make meaning for and digest, and that is good. Right, now it is time for second breakfast, as Pippin and Merry[2] would say!

A fair few years ago we were out on a course in southern Europe, Spain or Portugal I can't quite remember. One of the participants who was a teacher and ran his own dojo had been asked to give a demonstration of self-defence techniques. There were over two hundred delegates on the course, the majority of whom were Spanish and Portuguese but there was quite a large contingent of English. The teacher was very keen to impress such a large course, and particularly the participants from England. His English was just about adequate for the purpose of teaching the course. Towards the end of his demonstration, he

---
[2] Characters from the Tolkein novel, *The Lord of the Rings*, who seem to enjoy having breakfast more than once in a morning!!

wanted to demonstrate Kobutan[3] techniques. For some reason he didn't seem to want to use a Kobutan and asked for a pen. He said "the pen is mightier than a sword" in English, repeated it in Spanish, and then started his demonstration with a restraining technique. Unfortunately, during the demonstration the pen snapped in half. Now martial artists are known to like a bit of a joke, and never one to miss an opportunity, a bright spark piped up and said (in Spanish) "Shakespeare didn't have a biro," which resulted in a good deal of laughter. The following day we presented this teacher with a fountain pen, he took it from the box, rolled it in his fingers and said "If this snaps I can always stab them…. touché!".

Now have you bought a pad and paper yet, or a journal? I think we may have mentioned just how important it is that you do the exercises and write things down in previous chapters. If you don't yet have the necessary equipment, there is still time to pop out to the shops, after all this is a 24hr society and it is certainly incredible just what you can buy at petrol stations now. They are not just places to refuel, you can stock up on all manner of things.

So, our fine scholars of Hypnosis, the mind, and your inner selves, we have another exercise for you. It's back to school for a brief visit, but this time we are going in through the round window, were not using stun grenades or abseiling ropes though, we have much finer tools at our disposal. We are going to use your experience, a pen or pencil of your choice and a pad or a notebook (later you can type it up if you wish). We want you to write a letter to yourself, but first you need to start to build an appropriate vocabulary.

---

[3]The Kobutan is a palm hand baton, which is popular as a keyring with some martial artists.

> **Relaxing words: Do-it**
>
> *Relax*. This is a relaxing word isn't it? What other words do you know that are relaxing? Here are some examples:
>
> *Comfortable, drifting, soft, dreamy..*
>
> Write down as many relaxing words you can think of.
>
> Now, using a thesaurus or a dictionary of synonyms, write down at least 5 words that you could use instead of the word *relax*. Here are a couple of examples: *Unwind, let go.*

It is so important to have a rich vocabulary, and a variety and flexibility in the choice of words you use. And did you notice just how much more relaxed you can become when you say these dreamy, comforting, soothing words? Remember tonality? This is where it all goes together, the correct tone, and the correct vocabulary can generate the state that you want to generate. Just think how relaxed you might feel if I said to you "don't <u>be tense</u>, and your <u>shoulders</u> won't <u>hurt</u>". Compare this with, "Let the tension ease from your shoulders, and begin to replace it with a soothing and comforting feeling of relaxation."

Now that you have a rich vocabulary of relaxing words, it might be a good idea if you did the same with every state that you wanted to generate: excitement; happiness; motivation. It's just a thought. Let's put our relaxing words into practice:

> **A letter to yourself: Do-it**
>
> Write a letter to yourself, to your inner self, asking permission to for you to go to a safe place and relax. As you do this turn the paper 45 degrees to the left and write downward in three columns, for example:
>
> | | | |
> |---|---|---|
> | relax | yourself | now |
> | write | to | you |
> | now | relax | can |
> | you | in | relax |
> | can | the | more |
> | become | chair | than |
> | excitable | while | you |
> | allowing | you | were |
>
> Remember, read this down from the top to the bottom, starting at the top left hand word, relax. Now we would like to suggest that you now continue to do this several or many times each time using a wider and more varied vocabulary. For example after you have done the first one, can you do it again using a different word for *relax*?

As you may well have guessed, this chapter is all about language and about writing. We can't stress the importance of the process of practicing writing and using appropriate language enough. It is equally important that you begin to notice language, particularly in the media, in advertising, in the speeches of politicians and in your communications on a daily basis. We have already touched on this, but to make it absolutely clear, let's take an example of how the language that we use can have a powerful effect.

MAY WE SUGGEST?

I once watched, and overheard, a colleague of mine, a Kung Fu teacher, at a grading giving a pep talk to one of his students. This particular grading was in three parts, each of which counted equally: there was the form (Kata), the set techniques and the free fighting. This student had already performed his form, and his set techniques, and had barely done well enough (in the opinion of this teacher) to get through. Doing well in the free sparring was essential for this student to pass. From what I could tell, this performance level was unusual for the student, and the instructor put this down to nerves. I can't exactly remember the pep talk word for word, but I was sufficiently struck by it to recall snippets. It went as follows:

> "What is the matter with you? You're nervous aren't you? Don't think about how terrible you have already been, because if you are as bad as that in the fighting, you aren't going to pass. You want to pass don't you?" (The student nodded) "You can't afford to be crap in the fighting."

Can you guess what happened? Yes, the student was terrible, lost the fight, and stormed off the mat and out of the grading. It is clear that the language used by the instructor didn't have the desired effect. You probably get a gut feeling for that. But why exactly was it that this language didn't have the desired effect?

Well, one reason is that the entire sentence is predominantly negative. In order to think in the negative you have to first think in the positive. If you were asked not to think of a frog, you would probably have to think of a frog first in order to not think about it. Try this. Don't think of a purple orange. What happens? We will all think of something, but not many of us will do anything other than think of a purple orange. Most of us will have thought of a purple orange first, and then not think about it. In general, our subconscious minds ignore the negative, and go straight to the positive. Remember when you were a kid? "Don't feed the animals." What is the first thing that you would do?

The second reason is that within the pep talk of the teacher, there are a lot of embedded suggestions: *You are nervous; you have been terrible; you are bad; you aren't going to pass; be crap in the fighting.* This is of course not the message that the instructor wanted to put across. Nonetheless, it is there, embedded in the pep talk.

So the question is, how do you avoid making this mistake and make sure that the message that you do want to put across is in fact the one you put across?

Writing Suggestions

There are two types of suggestions: direct suggestions and indirect suggestions. *Indirect suggestions* are found in areas such as advertising, training and negotiating as well as in a form of Hypnosis known as permissive Hypnosis. They are also found all over the place, in our conversations and in our pep talks. You will be able to hear them, see them and read them everywhere when you start paying attention to what you are reading and hearing. The previous sentence is an example of indirect suggestion. Not so subtle examples are "Buy now, pay later" and "Smoking Kills".

From the perspective of Hypnosis, *direct suggestions* are most commonly used when trance has been achieved, because they appeal *directly* to the subconscious in an unambiguous and unconstrained way. However as the examples above show it is not necessary to be in a trance state to receive and integrate suggestions that are pretty unsubtle and direct. So how do you form good, positive suggestions?

- **Suggestions must be positive** - an example of a good positive suggestion is "Every day in every way I get better and better."
- **Suggestions must be progressive and may be continuous** – in other words they must refer to the present and future rather than the past. "You are going to continue to feel more comfortable"
- **Suggestions must be phrased simply and clearly** – the subconscious can't be bothered with sentences that are too complicated.

So for example, you could say:

> *You can improve, you have shown how good you are and you will be able to show that again and again. You have the ability.*

A pep talk: Do-it
Re-write the negative pep talk above using the rules of forming positive suggestions.
Now write your own motivation script.

SEE, FEEL, HEAR, RELAX NOW

Now that you have an idea about how to put the correct language into your scripts, and now that you have a rich vocabulary on which you can draw in order to build elegant, positive scripts that lead towards a state. It is almost time to put all of this into practice. But not yet, because as we have already said, it is important to practice, write, and think first as this will give you the confidence and flexibility when you perform your first official induction.

There is one further element, with which you are already very familiar. By combining your understanding of language with your understanding of the power of modalities and representation systems, you can build powerful relaxation and state inducing scripts. As an example, let's build a predominantly visually based relaxation script. First of all go back to your notes and look at your list of visual words, modalities and sub-modalities. You may have some of the following: *see, focus, perceive, bright, bold, colour, contrast*. Then find a relaxing context, for example lying on a beach in the sun, or sitting in a comfortable chair. Do make sure that whatever context you use, it is associated with the experience of relaxation. Finally create this experience by describing it and then noticing in detail what it is that you, or whoever it may be that you are writing the script for, saw at the time. The process of experiencing a relaxing state *inside* and focusing on the visual representation of that experience induces relaxation. An example script might be:

> *Perhaps you can remember sitting in a comfortable chair, relaxed, relaxing. Imagine yourself in that chair, and see what you saw. Notice the room around you, the colour of the walls, the carpet, the chair itself. Notice your hands, resting, comfortably; your fingers, your wrists, arms. Your chest rising and falling slowly, as you begin to drift into a dream-like state.*

In summary, here are the steps:

- Select the appropriate representation system (Visual, Auditory, Kinaesthetic – recall that different people have preferences for different systems and so the system you choose will depend on the person you are assisting).
- Find an appropriate context.

- Generate the experience of this context by using modalities and sub-modalities.
- Pepper your script with relaxing words at appropriate points.

Now it is time for you to practise. So get out your pen, and journal and do-it.

> **See, Hear, Feel: Do-it**
>
> Now we would like you to take the script above and expand it to a ten-minute visual relaxation script using only visual words
>
> Now write a ten-minute auditory relaxation script.
>
> Now a ten-minute kinaesthetic relaxation (how you feel)
>
> In order to ensure that you are using the appropriate amount of time, get an egg timer and time yourself as you speak

Now I wonder how easy you found it to do that. It is not easy to keep to one representation system. You may find the next do-it a lot easier now that you have been through the previous one. We are going to ask you to write a single ten-minute script, which combines all of the representation systems. You should be able to build this from the scripts you have already written. There is one specific idea that you need to bear in mind, and that is to do with the structure of the script. It is important to focus predominantly on one representation system at a time, and to find suitable places to *overlap*. For example building on the script above, notice how this one moves from the visual to the kinaesthetic system:

> *Perhaps you can remember sitting in a comfortable chair, relaxed, relaxing. Imagine yourself in that chair, and see what you saw. Notice the room around you, the colour of the walls, the carpet, the chair itself. Pay attention to your chest*

> *rising and falling... Slowly. Notice your hands, resting, comfortably; feel their weight, their warmth. Be aware of your back pressing against the chair, as you begin to drift into a dream-like state.*

See-Hear-Feel: Do-It

Now write a single ten-minute relaxation script, which uses all modalities and representation systems. Use the principle of overlap to switch seamlessly from one representation system to another.

Recently we were back in Spain and on a course with the same teacher. He was once again asked to do a demonstration (as he is a very fine teacher, you would certainly learn a lot training with him). With a flourish he produced the fountain pen we had given him and a large piece of paper. He called out of the group for someone to attack him and then, quick as a flash he unveiled the paper, which bore the legend "Shakespeare also had a sword." He turned the paper around, and the same thing was written in Spanish on the other side.

Touché!

Chapter 4 – Finding your own Doris

> *"Do not focus on a piece of what is going on; Feel your whole body. Feel the space around your body as well as what is going on infront of you. Feel your partners body and the space around that. Feel the two of you and the space around and in between, like two parts of one body. Fill the space between you with feeling pressure"*
> Ron Sieh, <u>Tai Chi Chuan, the Internal Tradition</u>.

THE WAY IN – ENTRANCE

He places the ball carefully, the same way that he has so many times before. Shutting out the cheers and jeers of the crowd, he stands up, and walks just the right amount of paces backwards. Then takes a single sidestep. But he is not yet ready. Standing with his feet a shoulder width apart, he clasps his hands in front of himself, staring at them for what seems like an age. Finally towards the posts, slightly upwards, he pulls his head back just a little, as if the target somehow magnifies in his vision. He focuses, and there he sees her, sitting right in the middle, in the crowd, between the posts. Then he feels it, he knows that he is ready. And the rest is history.

Johnny Wilkinson, the England rugby fly-half, always follows the same ritual every time he kicks for goal. He is one of the most successful kickers in the history of the game, and his cool head under stress helped the England team convert pressure into points and walk away with the Rugby World Cup in November

Grace Under Pressure

2003. The question is, how does he do it? Of course, the answer is not only in his constant practicing, but also in his ritual. By following this series of steps (which by now you should recognise as a series of anchors) he is able to get himself *in the zone* and shut himself away from all the pressure and noise. He has a single focus of attention, the process of kicking a rugby ball over the bar and between the posts. If you have a chance to watch him, you may also notice the defocusing of his eyes, and the flattening of his face, as he stares at his hands. More importantly, look at the way he looks up at the posts, bringing them closer in his mind, visualising the ball going up, and then down between the posts.

But Johnny attributes his success to one fact above all, that he is able to visualise a woman sitting in the crowd behind the posts, directly in-between them. He has named her Doris[4]. He aims for Doris, and invariably collects the three points on offer. Essentially, Johnny Wilkinson, England rugby player, hallucinates during his kicking process. Hallucination, along with a number of other phenomena that Johnny exhibits – single focus of attention, defocusing of the eyes, disassociation, and catalepsy[5] – are signs of trance. According to hypnotists of old (James 2000) positive hallucination (seeing things that aren't there) is an indicator of particularly deep trance. When he is at his most accurate, most elegant and most efficient, Johnny is in a brief, specifically directed trance.

---

4 Doris, in Greek mythology, is the goddess of gifts and giving, daughter of Gaia (the earth) and Okeanus (the rivers). Isn't this an interesting choice of name for such a prestigious hallucination?
5 Catalepsy is the experience of waxy stiffness in limbs. You may for example see someone with their arm up whilst they are asleep. Johnny Wilkinson demonstrates this when he clasps his hands together.

Finding Your Own Doris

And he isn't the only one. Other sporting greats work and train hard to be able to enter the zone exactly when they need to. It is so important that during the game, or performance attention is efficiently directed towards only one purpose, and motivation and energy are not wasted. In the zone baseball players report balls slowing down and growing in size, and golfers explain that the course shrinks. Athletes relate experiences of watching the race in slow motion whilst they themselves are in it. The really excellent sportsmen know when the time is right to strike the ball or throw a punch by a combination of being in the zone, and *feeling it*. When you throw a tennis ball in the air and hit it just right, in the sweet-spot, you feel that it is right, and you know how well the ball is going to fly. Great tennis players know that they are going to hit the ball in the sweet-spot *before* they throw it up in the air, because they recognise the feeling of it being *just right*.

Most of these sportspeople build a series of anchors, through ritual, to take them into the zone. Very much in the way that you did in the first chapter with the circle of power. As martial artists we use ritual to great effect to move from one state to another. The complicated etiquette, for example found in Kendo may not have been designed for the purpose, but by focussing entirely on the movements of your sword, and with excruciating exactitude on the position of the blade, your arm, your shoulder, your feet, you find yourself in a trance like state, perfect for the exquisite performance of an accurate and elegant Kata. The same is, of course, true of any Kata, or form. Take for example the twenty-minute Yang Tai-Chi long form. I always start the form in the same way, get part way through, and then find myself twenty minutes later having completed the form but not remembering the middle section at all, even though others tell me that I have completed it. This is similar to the experience of driving on a familiar route, and at some point finding yourself at home, having crossed three roundabouts and a T-Junction but not remembering anything about whole sections of the journey.

There are other good examples of trance, watching the TV for example, or reading a book. I drop into trance sitting on the train, trusting my subconscious to notice when it is time to get off. I have only ended up at the end of the line once, and that was after a particularly busy night out on the town. Even my subconscious gave up then!! The point is that trance is a naturally occurring phenomena, and once you know how to recognise it, is easy to spot all around you. It is particularly valuable as a way of focussing attention during sporting activities, and many excellent sportspeople use trance, or the zone (however you want to refer to this particular state) to enhance their performance.

The work that you have already done has lead you into trance many times, and if you followed our instructions you will have filmed yourself relaxing deeply, and watched it to see the signs of trance developing. In general everyone develops trance in their own way, but there are a few characteristics of trance that are relatively ubiquitous. A list follows, in no particular order. The easiest thing to remember is that the trance state is different from the waking state, and so anything that is different to behaviour in the waking state is potentially an indicator of trance.

Signs of Trance
- Flattening of the face
- Fluttering of the eyelids
- Defocusing of the eyes
- Twitching of the hands and feet
- Warmth in the hands, usually indicated by a redness as the blood comes to the surface
- Change in breathing, usually slower and deeper
- Drooping of the shoulders
- An asymmetry in the face

Finding Your Own Doris

And now it is time for your first do-it of this chapter. This is one of the most fun ones that you will get to do (of course they are all fun).

> **Noticing Trance: Do-it**
>
> This is a simple exercise, we want you to go out, and for a whole day, pay attention to people. In particular pay attention to people who are doing routine tasks, like shopping or typing, reading, sitting on trains and buses.
>
> See how many people you can identify as being in a trance, however briefly.
>
> In your club or class, look around. See if you can notice signs of trance in your students or seniors or juniors as they perform kata, sparring, grading practice.
>
> How about suddenly smiling at a shop assistant and saying "and you have a nice day too." See what happens.

How many of us have searched high and low for our keys, and not found them, only to discover them somewhere that we have looked before. Not seeing something that isn't there is known as negative hallucination and it is a phenomenon that is usually connected with deep trance. There is disagreement about the direct relationship between depth of trance and specific hypnotic phenomena. One school of thought suggests that you may only experience certain phenomena at a certain level of trance, and as a result demonstrating a particular phenomenon would indicate that depth of trance. This is plainly not true, as when we are looking for our keys we are clearly not in a deep trance. We subscribe to the other school of thought, which suggest that any trance phenomenon can be achieved in any state, waking or hypnotic.

It is certain, however, that some types of phenomena are easier to achieve at specific levels of trance, and that direct suggestion usually requires a medium to deep trance to be effective. You should note that not everyone can exhibit all phenomena, nor can they necessarily achieve all levels of trance. With these ideas in mind, the following table gives an indication of levels of trance and associated phenomena.

Level	Phenomena	
Light Trance	*Catalepsy*	– flexible rigidity in eyes and limbs
Medium Trance	*Amnesia*	– following suggestions to forget things
	Analgesia	– control of pain
Deep Trance Somnambulism	*Hallucinations*	
	Anaesthesia	– loss of feeling

AND IT ALL HAPPENS SO NATURALLY.

One of the most powerful ways of helping people to feel comfortable about going into a trance or experiencing various hypnotic phenomena is to use descriptions of universal experiences, such as those in the previous section (including Doris), to show that these behaviours are naturally occurring.

Naturally occurring states: Do-It
Take each of the following trance phenomena and write down two examples of where this occurs as a universal, naturally occurring state. For example, negative hallucination is often experienced when you can't see for looking!!
Catalepsy
Amnesia
Analgesia
Time Distortion

How did you do? It is in fact very easy to find examples of trance all over the place if you know where to look.

Catalepsy

The word catalepsy comes from the Doric (ancient Greek dialect spoken in Sparta) concept of *Katalepsis*, which was a phenomenon experienced in battle in which the soldier froze with fear, being possessed. The Spartans did not see that cataleptic behaviour was useful. However in the context of hypnosis, it can be extremely valuable.

When you try in vain to open your eyes but cannot, or show arm levitation without conscious effort, then you are exhibiting catalepsy. There is a sort of "waxy flexibility" in cataleptic parts of the body that allow, for example, an arm to stay up in the air for an unusually long time. Naturally occurring cataleptic states are in eating, when the fork is held up without food on it, expectantly, or perhaps when for some reason you don't want to move your head and keep your neck still without tension.

Time Distortion

Have you ever been driving at 70 along the motorway and when you pulled on to the slip road it seems as if you are going slowly enough, but you have to pull up rather sharply at the top? Or what about waiting for an important call, you seem to wait forever and then you look at your watch. Fast time; slow time. Wouldn't it be great if we could slow time down when we wanted? Then things we liked could last longer!! And speed it up too so that things we wanted to get over and done quickly seemed to do just that.

Analgesia and Anaesthesia

Where anaesthesia is the complete loss of sensation analgesia is the control of pain where the sensation of pressure is retained. Aspirins are analgesic, but Novocain is anaesthetic. Operations have been successfully performed under hypnosis, and this may be a combination of dissassociation and anaesthesia, as well as relaxation and stress relief. Knowledge of the feelings of analgesia are common as most people have taken pain control tablets, however more direct associations can be found with putting your hand in a bucket of ice, or noticing that your hand has gone to sleep. Anaesthesia is more difficult to recall, as it is often associated with loss of consciousness. Anyone who has had dental work or any other local anaesthetic will remember the spreading feeling of the numbness as the anaesthetic begins to work.

Dissassociation

This is where you have the sense of being detached from part of your body. Universal examples of this are when you see yourself on video or in a mirror. Disassociation often happens in dreams, and is useful for standing back and looking at a situation. Usually feelings linked to dissociated images are weaker than with associated ones. Disassociating is a good way of approaching phobias, or negative feelings.

Positive and Negative Hallucination

A *positive hallucination* is an hallucination that you have that everyone else would agree isn't there. Of course, if enough people agree with you that it is there, then it's true!! *Negative hallucination* is when you can't see something that is there (like my keys!!). Can you remember what a chocolate fudge brownie tastes like? Or how your favourite perfume smells? If you can, then you are hallucinating in the gustatory or olfactory senses respectively. How about not smelling something that everyone else agrees does smell - Negative hallucination. And what would you call it if you don't see something that isn't there? Normality?

Finding Your Own Doris

Amnesia

It's very easy and completely natural to forget. I don't know how many times I have forgotten things, sometimes unimportant things, or sometimes even important things only to remember them just at the right time. How often do you try to remember a phone number, even your own phone number? You don't until it is time to use it. Have you ever met someone, and forgotten their name soon afterwards? And when you go to the shops without a list, sometimes you forget some of the things that you went there for. Amnesia occurs everywhere, all the time to all of us. Let's face it, we just can't hold that much information in our heads at one time.

In fact this is one of the keys to inducing trance. George Miller (1952) wrote a seminal paper "the Magic Number 7 plus or minus 2", in which he explains the limits of the capacity of the human mind. Essentially we can hold in consciousness, between five and nine pieces of information MAXIMUM. Any more than that and we begin to get confused. Some induction methods use confusion and overloading to directly access the subconscious mind.

INTO THE UNKNOWN

This brings us nicely to the important question. Whatever is this thing that is sometimes referred to as the unconscious and sometimes the subconscious? How does it relate to the conscious mind (whatever that is)? In truth we don't know, all we can say in support of this division is that "it is presumptuous to claim that whatever goes on in the mind must be known to consciousness" (Freud 1915). What is important is that we *can* consider the mind as divided into two parts, and whether this is true or not, it is an effective model (metaphor) and one which helps us structure communications appropriately[6]. It is a distinction that makes Hypnosis possible, and allows us to make sense of the way that we are able to run automatic processes, such as breathing, walking, keeping our heart beating, driving and talking. We know that it is the neural system that keeps these automatic processes running, and we also know that we are not consciously aware (not until our attention is somehow drawn to it) of them.

Just think for a moment about the time you learnt a specific technique, perhaps a kick, or a way to strike a ball, something that is broken down into steps. Each step is taught independently, and then little by little combined into a single movement. If felt perhaps awkward, unnatural at first and then the movements became more and more familiar until suddenly you can just do it, whenever you want, more and more accurately every time, without thinking. At this point the process has become automatic, unconscious. In fact so automatic that it may even become difficult to break it back down into steps in order to teach it. It is this process, the process of breaking an activity or task into small steps and then repeating it until it becomes a single complete unconscious automatic process, which is used to teach physical skills and build *muscle memory*. In martial arts we are particularly good at this, and training is geared towards this aim, the aim of building a successful strategy for making movement unconscious. It is important in a combat situation to be able to react instantly *without thinking*. So often these unconscious processes save lives or win competitions.

---

[6] We will see this a little later on.

Finding Your Own Doris

> **What does the unconscious do? Do-It.**
>
> This is a simple exercise, all you have to do is take a clean piece of paper and divide it into two parts. As a heading write <u>Conscious</u>, on one half and <u>Unconscious</u> on the second half. Now write a list of functions of each part of the mind underneath.
>
> For example the unconscious is *automatic* while the conscious is *deliberate* and the unconscious is *intuitive* while the conscious is *logical*. See what else you can come up with (there are more examples in an appendix).

SO WHERE IS YOUR DORIS?

Now we have explored the unconscious, and we have seen the signs of trance. You may even be able to recognise the signs of trance around you and in more formal situations. We have also seen that trance is a very valuable activity and in particular is related to the sporting phenomena of going into the zone. And we have explored the strategy of Johnny Wilkinson as he kicks for goal. Apparently the key to Johnny's success is that he practises constantly, even on Christmas Day, and to the exclusion of everything else. But he doesn't only practice kicking, he practises the entire ritual, from the moment he enters a trance state, through his hallucination of the now (in)famous Doris to the unconscious completion of the kick. He has built and practised a strategy for success, and then repeated this strategy until it became a natural, automatic process at the unconscious level, just like breathing or speaking, or reading.

And here is the key to success in every activity, physical, social and cerebral. Establish a strategy, find your Doris and practise repeatedly until the strategy becomes automatic. Let's try it.

Grace Under Pressure

> **Unconscious strategy: Do-It**
>
> Identify a skill that you would like to improve, or learn. Watch videos of this skill being performed by experts, read books and devise a strategy for carrying it out. Write the strategy in your journal as a numbered list. Like this:
>
> **Front Kick**
>
> Focus on target
>
> Bring target closer
>
> Rotate hip towards front
>
> Raise knee to chest etc.
>
> You now need a way of checking that everything feels right, your Doris. This could be a feeling, or it could be something that you see. Perhaps you get tunnel vision, or maybe it just feels right. In the example of the kick above, for example, see the target area go red when you know that it is time to kick. At that point, begin the process...
>
> Whatever you choose to be your check, activate it now. And slowly go through the strategy. Check again, does it still feel right? Repeat this process until you have built a muscle memory, and connected skill with the strategy and the check.

Martial arts teaching capitalises extremely well on notions of trance and building unconscious strategies, and sportsmen, professional and amateur, use trance to learn new strategies and perform at their best. I once knew of a student who, during a demonstration was showing knife self-defence. He was attacked a number of times by assistants with live (very sharp) blades, and each time defended correctly, executing perfect technique. There was a lot of applause for this dangerous and spectacular demonstration. As we walked to the edge of the mat, he noticed that there was blood on him, and both he and I looked around to find out who it had come from, thinking that one of the attackers had been cut. And then we noticed that it had come from his own arm. He had been so much in the zone that he didn't notice that he had been cut, nor how deep the wound was. What was also amazing was that we had no idea when he had been cut, as there was no evidence of bleeding during the demonstration, and in fact the amount of blood was very small for such a wound. Of course, we went to hospital, and they decided to stitch. You have never heard such complaints!! Especially when you compare the size of the needle with the great big knife that had taken a chunk out of his arm.

Chapter 5 – Knowing where you are heading

"It is favourable to have in view some goal or destination, and to cross the great sea."
Hexagram 42. I (Yee) GAIN, <u>I-Ching</u>.

GET SMART, AND THEN SOME

There was once a student of ours, a very good student, who seemed to always find that there was something very important to do whenever it came to an important grading. He would put in all of the work, come along to the extra classes, work on his fitness, his form, his weaponry, his technique. But as it came closer to the grading he would suddenly find that something had come up that would prevent him from attending. And this was his black belt grading. His juniors were passing him by, and becoming black-belts band teachers, while he continued preparing for his grading. He was beyond the required standard, but never attending a grading and never graded. It got to a point where he was no longer progressing, he had peaked and if he didn't manage to take his grading soon, he would go off of the boil. In fact in the past, he *had* gone off of the boil, and taken a year or so out of training. But now he was back, and he wanted to take the grading (or so he said) but there was something missing - him, from the grading!!

Now, as a teacher and coach, you have responsibilities to your students, not only to teach them what it is that they need to know, but also to motivate, enthuse, counsel and encourage. But by the same token, students need to be driven to achieve their own goals, not by pressure from the coach, but by compulsion from within. But then this student did seem to be driven; he was certainly motivated enough to attend all of the extra training, and he was a quality martial artist. In fact it was becoming an embarrassment to have him as a 1st Kyu (brown-belt), as he was much better than some of his seniors.

More than once I had sat down with him, and chatted to him about his goals, where he saw himself and how he hoped to progress. I had even asked if there was anything else that he thought may help him go forwards, and I wondered what I could do to help him get to the grading. Usually he would say, "I'm fine thanks, it's just a question of organisation". But I knew it wasn't. So eventually, in an effort to get to the bottom of this, I invited him round to my house for a cup of tea. I said that I wanted to help him achieve his goal of becoming a black-belt, and I wondered if he would consider spending some time looking at how he and I could do something that would help him get there. He came round on a Tuesday evening, and I made tea. The dialog went something like this:

> *Me*: ""*I notice that you are having difficulty in managing to get to the gradings. I am wondering if you really do want to ever take your black-belt or not. So let me ask you, what exactly do you want to achieve?*"
>
> *Student*: "*I do want to get my black-belt*"
>
> *Me*: "*And when you have your black-belt, what will that mean to you*"
>
> *Student*: "*I will be much more confident*"
>
> *Me*: "*About what?*"
>
> *Student*: "*Just in myself, generally*"

Knowing Where You Are Heading

Me: "So you want to get your black-belt to be more confident?"

Student: "Yes"

Me: "So do you need more confidence right now?"

Student: "Yes, I suppose so"

Me " Well you must do, since you have said that after you have passed your black-belt you will have more Confidence"

Student: "Well that's right. I don't really have the confidence in my ability, or in general, anywhere"

Me: "Anywhere? Do you have the confidence that you are a good brown-belt?"

Student: "Yes of course"

Me: "But you didn't have the confidence that you are good enough to be a black-belt?"

Student: "That's right"

Me: "So its really the other way round then isn't it? You need some more confidence in order to take your black belt, and when you have sat, and passed that grading you will then be able to look back and see how easy it was, and how good you now are, and how much more confidence you have."

Student: "yes"

Me: "So what you are saying is that in order to pass your grading, you need more confidence that you can do it, and once you have done it, you will have more confidence. Let me ask you this. What is the purpose of taking your grading and becoming a black-belt?"

Student: "To prove that I can do it...To give me more self-confidence"

Me: "Ok, I understand. What would happen if you already had that confidence, would you still take the grading?"

Student: "Yes, of course, because I would know I could do it".

Me: "Yes you do. Let me summarise then. Your real goal is not actually to pass your black belt, it is to have more self-confidence. And when you do have more self-confidence then you know you will be able to achieve, as a by *product, your black belt, which will serve as confirmation that you have achieved your real goal. Am I right?"*

Student: *"I suppose you are, I have never thought of it like that, but yes, you are right"*

Me: *"Well, self-confidence we CAN do, right here, right now. Let's start by expressing your goal in a useful way. Are you happy for us to proceed?"*

So I had got to the bottom of the problem, it was essentially a self-confidence issue. There are a number of ways to deal with this sort of problem, and you may notice that in the dialogue above I had already begun the process. We will follow this process through, with this student, during the next few chapters. This student had mixed his goal up: what he was aiming for, and what was an obstacle weren't actually the right outcomes. It is so important that when you are expressing an outcome, or thinking of strategies to achieve a goal, that they are the right ones. And then you have to make sure that you express them in a valuable and useful way.

There is a lot of confusion between the terms *aim*, *goal* and *outcome*. And it is not at all an easy distinction to make. Aims however, are general and at a high level. Something like "I want to win". This is a laudable aim, but with such an aim it is not clear how we can ever achieve it, as this aim is complex with many constituent parts. The only way to achieve this aim is to break it down into smaller, more manageable goals. For example you may notice that a particular aspect of your sport is weak, say your hip throw, and you may set yourself the goal of turning making 75% of your hip throws in competition into ippon or wazari. Or you may notice that your putting is not always on-line, you may set yourself the goal of making 95% of your 10 Yd putts. It is important to think of goals *as memories of the future* (Liggett, 2002).

Jarvis (1999) divides goals into two types, **performance** goals and **outcome** goals. A performance goal would focus on an area of performance, and an outcome goal would focus on a specific outcome, such as winning a competition, or passing a grading. In general performance goals, because they are more specific, are better than outcome goals. We think that it is helpful to make one further distinction, between goals and outcomes themselves. The outcomes of a goal are specific, measurable, immediate and achievable. A number of outcomes make up a goal (a performance goal or an outcome goal) and a number of goals make up an aim. As a coach, trainer or teacher you may like to ask yourself the following questions when setting goals:

1. What is the purpose of this piece of teaching? (**Goal**)
2. Why do I want to do it? (**Aim**)
3. How can I help my students achieve this goal? (**Outcomes**)
   (adapted from Rogers(1998 p.123))

What are your goals: Do-It
This is a simple do-it. Now you know the difference between goals, outcomes and aims, write down a number of your aims, no more than three. Now break each of these into goals, and each goal into outcomes.
You should have a list of perhaps 10 – 20 outcomes, and maybe 5 –10 goals.

There are a number of ways of checking how well you have written of your outcomes. And there are a lot of recommendations for the way in which you should express them. In our experience the SMART approach makes writing outcomes simple (as long as you follow the guidelines) and the well-formedness conditions (McDermott 2000) take SMART outcomes and make them into outcomes that are most valuable and achievable.

SMART outcomes are:

Specific – This distinguishes aims from outcomes. For example, you may aim to be the best at your sport or art, but in order to do this you need to specify a number of specific outcomes, such as making my front kick 10% more powerful, or driving 10 more meters every swing.

Measurable – There is no point in setting yourself an outcome without clear criteria that allow you so see whether you have achieved it or not. Outcomes like, "I want to be able to punch 15% more powerfully" are excellent, as it is very simple to know when you have achieved them or not.

Achievable – It goes without saying that you should set outcomes that are within the limit of ability. Roger Bannister set himself the 4-minute mile, but he didn't set himself the 3-minute mile. It is unlikely that you will ever play golf like Tiger Woods (unless you are Tiger Woods, in which case would you mind endorsing this book?), but you can improve your game by 10 or 15 percent. Then again don't make them too easy -more difficult goals take more effort but have more eventual benefit. It is all about balance.

Realistic – Going hand in hand with the Achievable criteria, realistic goals are those that are achievable by someone. It is not very sensible to set the goal of flying to the moon with a Hang glider.

Timely – And here is where goals become outcomes. Outcomes are immediate, or at least have a time component. Goals don't. So a good SMART goal is: *to improve your hip throws, to be* *measured by an increase in the numbers of throws that score points in competitions by 50%, over the next three months.*

SMART Outcomes: Do-It

This do-it is about writing SMART outcomes. Take one of your goals. It could be connected with training or anything else. How could that be expressed more accurately as a series of SMART outcomes? The way to do this is to take piece of paper (journal page) and write the goal (be more confident) at the top of it. Then write the letters S.M.A.R.T down the side. And then go through them asking is it Specific? Is t Measurable? Etc. If it isn't modify the goal at each stage until you get to the end.

For example your goal may be to have more motivation

S – is this specific? No. Change to; *To have more motivation to go training*

M – Measurable? No. *To increase my motivation to go training to 95%. To be measured by my attending all training sessions*

A – Achievable? – Yes, except on my birthday which is in two week's time, and I would rather go to the pub then. Change to: *To increase my motivation to go training to 80%. To be measured by my attending 4 out of 5 training session.*

Can you see how this works? Continue with the above example, and then do your own.

So now you are SMART, but are you well formed? SMARTly specifying outcomes is a good start but it leaves out some of the key elements that can really lead to success. The well-formed outcome criteria are the place that the art of writing positive suggestions and SMART outcomes come together. They also allow outcomes to be set that work particularly well in a coaching and hypnotic framework.

Well-formed outcomes...

- Are stated in the positive, and are specific (the S of SMART).

- Specify the outcome in terms of what you will see, hear and feel when you have achieved it.

- Identify the evidence that will convince you that you have achieved it (the M or Smart)

- Consider the context that this outcome will occur in. Answering the questions where, when and with whom do you want this outcome (the T or SMART).

- Consider the purpose and consequences of the outcome. Why do you want it, what will it do for you and what will it do for others (The AR of SMART) ?

- Identify the resources that you need in order to get from where you are now, to where you want to go.

By taking a goal, turning it into an outcome and running it through the well-formedness check, you are already well on the way towards achieving that goal. Let's continue our discussion with the student.

Me: So you want to be more confident? You want to have more confidence, enough in fact to give you the strength to go to the grading? And when you have passed the grading that will boost your confidence even more.

Student: *Yes*

Me: So how will you know that you are confident enough?

Student: *To do what?*

Knowing Where You Are Heading

Me: To do whatever. I mean how will you feel? What will you see, or hear?

Student: What do you mean? ... er...I suppose I'll feel more confident.

Me: And how does that feel? ...Can you remember a time when you were really confident (waits)...that's right...now tell me is there a feeling associated with that? ..Yes...what does it feel like.

Student: Warm

Me Warm...Good. And when you have that confidence what will you hear?

Student: .Like people you mean? Talking to me about how positive I am?

Me: That's right. So where do you want to have these feelings of confidence?

Student: Well, before the grading...but..

Me: And after the grading, and everywhere? Is there anywhere that you wouldn't want his confidence?

Student: No, not really. I just want to be more confident, everywhere.

Me: So how confident are you now?

Student: Not very.

Me: And what do you think you need to help give you all the confidence you need? How much more confidence do you need?

Student: Well I probably need twice as much.

> **Well Formed Outcomes: Do-It**
>
> Can you go through the dialogue above and identify where I have asked the well formedness questions?
>
> Now take each of the well formedness criteria and write it as a heading on your page. Go through the dialog above and under each heading write the way in which the outcome that we have defined, being confident, satisfies each criteria.
>
> For example:
>
> *Specify the outcome in terms of what you will see, hear and feel when you have achieved it.*
>
> The student will feel warm, and will hear people praising his confidence.
>
> Now use the well-formedeness criteria to re-write your own SMART goals

ARE YOU LICKING YOUR LIPS YET?

Now that we have our SMART outcomes and we are sure that they are well formed, we have to make them compelling. Richard Bandler, one of the founders of NLP, says that unless you are licking your lips then the goal isn't compelling enough. You already have all of the tools you need to be able to take goals and make them desirable and attractive, and we will show how to use them here.

Submodalities (Chapter 2), if you recall, can help you intensify feelings and magnify desires about events in the future (and in the past). It's a simple step then to take an outcome, and make it more compelling by working with the submodalities. By turning up the brightness, making it bolder, clearer, by adding a soundtrack, turning up the volume and pushing it just far enough out into the future. In fact, haven't you already done exactly this, in

Knowing Where You Are Heading

the circle of power ? Here you can see how everything is beginning to come together.

There is one key submodality that you need to focus on when thinking about goals and outcomes. If you think about a compelling outcome, and adjust the submodalities until you find yourself licking your lips, and then make sure that you are in the picture, looking through your own eyes, totally associated with the experience, then you may get a sense of completion, a sense that the goal has already been achieved. *It is better to see yourself in the picture*, to be disassociated. This gives you more of a sense that the goal is yet to be achieved, that you need to work towards it, making it even more compelling, making you want it even more. Let's see, feel and hear how this works.

> *Me: So you want to be more confident? Can you think of a time when you were confident?*
>
> **Student**: Yes...I suppose so..
>
> *Me: But are you sure? It doesn't have to be a time connected with training, it could be anything.*
>
> **Student**: Yes. I have got it
>
> *Me: Ok. Can you see yourself in that event?*
>
> **Student**: Yes.
>
> *Me: Ok now notice the characteristics of the picture. Is it Bright or Dark? Colour or black and white? Fuzzy or clear? A movie or a still?*
>
> **Student**: Colour, movie...bright.
>
> *Me: And if you make it brighter, how much more confident do you feel?*
>
> **Student**: It is better, yes.
>
> *Me: And bolder ? And how about if you add a soundtrack? What is your favourite "confident" music?*
>
> **Student**: Got it. Yes I am feeling more confident.

Me: Excellent. Now, make a picture of a time in the future in which you think that you will need this confidence. In fact make a few. Now put the others to the side and pick one. Now make the picture brighter, make it a movie, make it bolder, add your confident sound-track... Now push it out into the future, just as far as it needs to be. Make sure you are seeing yourself in it. How do you feel about that event now?

Student: Good. Like I can do it.

Me: Great. Now put all of these future events in a line, out in your future. Make each one as compelling as the one you have just made. You know, make them brighter, and bolder, a movie, colourful... How do you feel now, now that you know that you have as much confidence as you need?

Compelling goals: Do-it

And now it is your turn. Take one of your goals or outcomes (make sure that it is well formed, and SMART).

Visualise the outcome. Make sure that you are watching yourself in the outcome. Now adjust the submodalities to make it more compelling. You may have had an experience in the past where you had this resource, if so you can re-experience it and elicit your submodalities for this particular resource from it. If not, just change the submodalities until it is more and more compelling.

Anchor this state so that you can re-experience it anytime you like. In the example above, the word "Confidence" served as the anchor.

Now push it out into the future. Make it both compelling and achievable.

Don Liggett (2002) points out that in his experience, goal setting is easier while the subject is in trance. He suggests that this may be because the subconscious mind (which he connects with the right brain) has a clearer idea of the capabilities than the conscious mind. This is something you may like to try. Perhaps you will come up with even more compelling and challenging goals.

Knowing Where You Are Heading

So now we have arrived. You have a list of compelling goals, you understand about submodalities, naturally occurring trance states, anchors and writing suggestions. You may not have realised it yet, but throughout this book you have been experiencing many different versions of trance states, and you may have induced them in others already. In the next chapter we will introduce formal processes for inducing trance, and look at elegant ways of using language to guide individuals and groups into hypnotic states in which you can make even better use of your tools.

Chapter 6 – Challenge YOU the trance

> *The only way that you can understand consciousness is in relation to yourself; it is the awareness of your being.... It is your self within yourself...*
> Ormand McGill. <u>The Secrets of Dr Zomb</u>

LET ME TELL YOU HOW

One day, whilst chatting to a friend, he asked me how it was possible to hypnotise someone, how I would do it. I said that it is really quite simple, but that it is not a case of hypnotising anyone, that the hypnotist is more of a guide really, helping you go down into deeper and deeper states of relaxation in which you can begin to work on the issues that you want to work on or have learnings and understandings at a subconscious level, bypassing your critical mind and allowing things to take place, all by themselves.

"You see", I continued, "now that you are becoming comfortable, all that your guide has to do is to help you become more aware of things that you weren't perhaps previously aware of. Like for example the warmth in your left hand, or the rising and falling of your chest as you breathe ever more slowly and comfortably. When helping someone go down, even deeper into trance as they listen to the soothing sound of my voice, feeling certain sensations, they may find that their eyelids begin to feel heavy and that the relaxation that begins around their eyelids starts to float down, as they do, from the top of their head to the tip of your toes. And as it floats, drifting, all the way, down now, the relaxation in your shoulders, arms, chest, legs, feet. You float. All the way down. As far as you need to go now in order to rest. And that's how easy it would be". I said.

AND NOW YOU CAN RELAX, BIT BY BIT

It really is simple to induce trance, in individuals or groups. The key is to take the approach that trance is a gift from the hypnotist to the subject, and that if it is offered it must be taken willingly or not at all. Hypnosis is not a fight, and there is no sense in struggling with a challenge offered by someone who purports to be un-hypnotisable. The subject is always and totally in control of how far into trance they go, and for how long they stay. Hypnosis is relaxing, restful and therapeutic. It is your job as guide to create an environment where they can stay as long as they wish and need to, in a relaxing restful state. The hypnotic state is one in which the conscious mind gives space to the subconscious in order to allow the changes and learnings and understandings and work to take place. So with a willing subject, how do you proceed?

In this book, we are focusing on the applications of Hypnosis in sports and martial arts, and as such the inductions that we will use are specifically relevant for these activities. However they are equally relevant to any form of therapeutic hetero- or self-Hypnosis. Hetero hypnosis is the process of hypnotising someone else, and you will be shown two straightforward methods of doing just this. Finally, we will show you how to build flexible inductions by combining these two approaches.

Before we start, there is time for a note on flexibility. Some hypnotists will read a standard script when inducing trance, often called a "patter". Some hypnotists profess to use 100 different methods of induction, but in reality use the same method in over 100 different ways. There are a good number of different ways to induce hypnosis and they essentially fall into two camps. *Direct hypnosis* uses direct suggestion, and commands, instructing the client to become hypnotised. On certain people this works extremely well. *Indirect hypnosis* uses a permissive approach, with indirect suggestion and may or may not use a formal trance induction at all. Everyone is different, and even the most willing subjects may not be able to follow your instructions if those instructions don't match their personality. And certainly very few people will respond to a monotonous tone and read or recited scripts (after all what would be the difference between this and buying a CD or tape?). Flexibility in approach allows you to tailor your induction to the client, and modify your approach in response to them as the induction progresses. However when you are starting out, it is handy to have a basic structure, and the following progressive relaxation induction is both a valuable framework that you will continue to use and evolve as you grow and develop as a hypnotist, and a basic patter script if you wish to memorise it completely (which we do not really recommend).

Progressive Relaxation

The progressive relaxation scheme essentially works by taking one part of the body (usually the eyelids) and showing that it can be relaxed to such an extent that it just doesn't seem to want to work. And then moving that relaxation from the top down to the bottom (head to feet), or from the bottom up to the top (feet to head), allowing each muscle group to relax in the same way until the entire body is relaxed. When the body is relaxed then the mind is relaxed in a similar way, until complete relaxation is achieved. This method induces light to medium trance states, which are perfectly adequate for most types of healing trance work, however a suitable deepener could be used to increase the depth of trance if required. The following script outline will help you to formulate your own progressive relaxation script.

- Relax one part of the body.
- Use direct suggestion to make that part of the body so relaxed that it just won't work. Heavy. Tired.
- Make subject acutely aware of that relaxation.
- Now take the relaxation and move it slowly throughout the body, up or down, mentioning each part of the body that is to be relaxed by name.
- Now relax the mind. Explain that this means that you leave everything and the mind becomes quiet.
- Count down from 101, backwards (in threes!) until the numbers disappear and the subject can't count anymore.

The following is an example of a script for a top down approach:

Progressive relaxation script example

> I want you to close your eyes, and direct your focus to your eyelids, and the muscles around your eyelids.
>
> Now relax the muscles around your eyelids until you are sure that they are so relaxed that they just won't work
>
> Now take that relaxation and move it through your body, relaxing first the muscles in your cheeks, around your face…... your neck…. shoulders...
>
> And allow the relaxation to move down towards your feet, inch by inch, ion by ion, and as it does...
>
> And now that you are completely relaxed I want you to begin the process of relaxing your mind, just relax it so far that you just leave everything , just allow things to disappear, just for a moment
>
> I want you to begin counting in your mind, down from 101, begin counting slowly and after each number you will double your mental relaxation..
>
> and at some point you won't be able to remember where you are where you have got to,...and it won't

Challenge YOU the Trance

> *matter and it will show you just how relaxed your mind has become...*
> *begin...One Hundred and One ...double the relaxation... 100...double ....drifting ....floating ....etc...*
> *and let them fade away to nothing...*

It is important to use a relaxed tone and intersperse relaxing words in your induction.

And then what?

We will discuss in the next chapter the best ways of utilising an hypnotic state (commonly this is known as an "intervention") , but there are simple things that you can say to make trance worthwhile, not just as an exercise in relaxation. This is the notion of 'content free' intervention, in which all specifics are removed from suggestions, so that the client/ subject is free to allow their mind to wonder (and wander) wherever they like and work on whatever they wish, if they wish to. This method is often used as a specific intervention approach by therapists as it prevents interference and potential problems that could be caused by taking someone where they don't feel comfortable. In general one should take care that this doesn't happen when speaking to a subject in trance.

For the purpose of the following exercises, you will be taking subjects into a trance state and bringing them back. This simple content free script will help you help them, continue to help them feel comfortable, and allow them to enjoy the trance (they may even volunteer again!!).

> *"...And now rest, relax, and allow your unconscious mind to work on whatever it needs to, or to just refresh... (pause)..*

Grace Under Pressure

Not difficult, yet extremely powerful, and totally content free.

You will probably now be wondering what you should do when you want to bring someone out of trance. There are many approaches, and you have probably seen the traditional Hypnotist counting back from five and saying things like "as I count back from 5 to 1 you will come out of trance more with every number I count". This is a perfectly legitimate and effective method, which with one modification we may even use ourselves. When counting someone *down* into trance we recommend counting *down* from 5 to 1, when counting someone *up* out of trance we recommend counting *up*, from 1 to 5. This simple modification can eliminate all sorts of confusions.

However our usual approach is not to force people out of trance (as is often found with the counting back method) but rather to ask them to return when they have finished, and are ready. You will normally find that the return is pretty quick. There is no risk that someone will stay in trance forever, and if they do refuse to come out it is usually because they are having such a wonderful time; just leave them to drop into a relaxing sleep, they will wake up eventually. However you will want to start the process and help your subject back to the here and now. The following lines will be enough:

> *"Now, in your own time, come back to the here and now..., only as quickly as you are ready to return. "*

And now that you have the basic building blocks; let's try your first formal induction.

> **Relaxation induction do-it**
>
> Take the basic framework of the progressive relaxation induction above and write out a complete script. Remember to use relaxing words. You should already have a list of these.
>
> Now find a willing "client" and practice. Read the script, or better still, use the script as a framework and make up an induction as you go along.
>
> Use smooth transitions between sentences. For example keep related ideas together. "Relax the muscles around your eyes, and now in your cheeks", rather than relaxing eyes and then straight down to feet!!
>
> When your client is in a light trance, say
>
> *" and now rest, relax, and allow your unconscious mind to work on whatever it needs to , or to just refresh... (pause)...*
>
> and when they seem to have had enough time to work at the subconscious level, invite them back.
>
> *"Now, in your own time, come back to the here and now...only as quickly as you are ready to return. "*

The progressive relaxation method is an excellent, simple and effective way of inducing hypnosis. However it doesn't offer quite as much flexibility as other methods. As we have suggested, everyone responds to hypnosis in different ways. And as a busy martial artist, sportsman or coach you will know that it pays to have a variety of approaches for the myriad of possible situations that can occur. That flexibility is offered by an elegant and simple set of patterns, first formally identified in the inductions of Milton Erickson (Bandler and Grinder 1975) although used unconsciously for years by competent hypnotists, and now found in sales training everywhere. This is the concept of truisms.

YES, YES, YES...

A truism is a statement that you make or a question that you ask whose answer you know already, and the answer is usually "Yes". The use of this type of language is an elegant and efficient way of pacing and leading just through the language you use. Truisms give a link between the experience that the client is having and the experience that the client will be having next, leading them from one state to the next. For example:

> *You are sitting there, listening to me, as you begin to relax*

It is undisputed that you are sitting there (as long as you are) and that you are listening to me, but you may not be aware that you are relaxing. In fact you may not be relaxing until the embedded command "begin to relax" is given.

Here are a few more truisms, on their own, for you to use later.

> *You can hear the sound of my voice.... You feel your feet pressing against the ground....your back against the chair..., your eyelids are heavy......your shoulders are relaxing...... your eyes are closed...... you become aware of the warmth in your left hand.... Your palms resting against your thighs... as you listen to something...while you become aware of certain positive and valuable things..*

Truisms divide into two main classes: *internal* and *external*. External truisms are those that are externally observable or verifiable *"your hands are resting on your lap"*, *"you can hear the music."* Internal truisms are truisms that can only be verified by the client, **by going inside themselves**, thereby deepening their own trance, such as *"you will learn something"* and *"you can sense certain things"*

Take for example this statement:

> *You can place your hands on your knees, and as you hear my voice you can listen to something else, and you can wonder just how deeply into trance you will be able to go.*

Here we have a number of external truisms – *hands placed on knees, hear my voice* – then internal truisms – *you can listen to something else, you can wonder.* Notice too the way in which the statement paces (where you are - *hands on knees, listening*) and then leads (where you are going - *deeply into trance*).

Perhaps you also remember Chapter 4 in which we looked at very similar statements, concentrating on the different representation systems. This is a standard process for using yes sets: to start in one representation system, and cross over to another. Pacing for example, kinaesthetic, and then leading into visual:

> *You can feel the sensations of the chair on your back, and the weight of your eyelids as your eyes close, and you become aware of the curious colours on the insides of your eyelids, while you begin to bring to mind positive images ...*

Yes Sets: Do-It
Can you identify the internal and external statements amongst the set of example truisms at the start of this chapter?
Write down 5 truisms that are EXTERNAL – statements that can be verified. Example: *You are sitting.*
Write down 5 truisms that are INTERNAL – statements that cannot be externally verified. Example: *You are thinking.*

The rule of three

Putting groups of truisms together is known as forming a "yes set". There is a simple rule for yes sets, and following it has a powerful effect. You will recognise this rule in action in advertising you, will see it in direct sales techniques. You can even use it on your boss if you want a rise. Why don't you try? The rule is: *If you make three statements that someone else can agree with easily, the fourth statement can be a command or a direct suggestion which has a very high chance of being followed.* For example, do you recognise this pattern?

1. You want a car that is safe.	...(don't you?) 1st Truism
2. You want a car that is economical to run.	...(don't you?) 2nd Truism
3. You want a car that is comfortable to drive.	...(don't you?) 3rd Truism
You want the XYZ car.	**COMMAND**

So how does this work in the induction process?

A yes set induction outline

- You may pick anything that is undeniably true of the client (in group work you should pick something that applies to everyone, universals, we will touch on this a little later on). This builds rapport.
- Connect the statements with *while, and, as*.
- Insert direct suggestions after a suitable number (3) of truisms.
- Gradually increase the number of direct suggestions and reduce the number of (external) truisms.

Here are two simple examples of yes sets:

You can look at your arm, and see your watch on your wrist; as you look at that watch you can feel it on

> *your wrist, you feel it and you become aware of its weight as it begins to feel heavier and heavier.*
>
> *While you continue tapping your foot on the ground and are hearing the music in the background I can begin to talk to you and you can listen to my voice.... Now you can feel the chair pressing against your back, and become curiously aware of your feet against the rung of the chair as you start the process of relaxing*

You may find them useful in the next do it..

The *Countdown yes set* Induction method

This is a very straightforward way of using truisms to induce trance. It essentially follows the outline above, but gives you a more defined process for building inductions (should you require it). First you start with 4 truisms, and one direct suggestion, then go to 3 truisms followed by 2 direct suggestions, then 2 and 3, and 1 and 4...

Remember, in order to make this, and other yes set inductions even more effective, take care to move your truisms from external initially (*hands on knees*) to internal (*you can wonder*). For example:

> *You can place your hands on your knees, and as you hear my voice you can listen to something else, and you can wonder just how deeply into trance you will be able to go.*

More Yes Sets: Do-It

Take the list of yes sets that you made in the previous do-It and, using the outline, write an induction script. You may like to use the countdown method, at least initially as this will help to give structure to your script. Remember to always start externally and move to the internal with your truisms.

> (...)
> You will find all the yes sets you need already in the examples in this chapter; all you have to do is put them together.
>
> Try out your script on a willing subject. Remember, after they are in trance, say to them something along the lines of *"and now you can use this time to rest, or work at the subconscious level on something that is important to you. And when you are ready, in your own time, come back to the here and now refreshed and invigorated."*
>
> And bring them out in the usual way.

THE COMBINATION METHOD

The final method of induction that we will introduce here combines both the yes set and the progressive relaxation script into one. It offers the flexibility and the rapport building of the yes set, and the structure of the progressive relaxation. Of course, when you combine two extremely effective methods of induction together, you get a very powerful, very flexible, very effective induction method that is perfect for groups and individuals. One outline of the process is as follows:

Outline of the combination method

Yes Set	You are sitting in the chair, listening to me, breathing, as your eyelids become heavier and heavier..
Relax body	...as you begin to relax, and take that relaxation down from your eyes …. (continue here with the relaxation script)
Yes set	And your legs are feeling heavy, your arms are feeling heavy, you are so relaxed and heavy...
Relax mind	And now that your body is completely relaxed you are going to relax your mind,... (counting down and losing numbers)
Yes Set	Your mind is completely relaxed, the numbers have faded, and your unconscious is ready for you to go even deeper...
Deepener	And now you may continue with an appropriate deepener (see section below)

The basic principle is to combine the rapport building and pacing and leading of the yes set with continuing suggestions of relaxation. Remembering the following basic principles, summarised here and covered elsewhere in this chapter, you can build any number of inductions by interspersing relaxation suggestions within groups of yes sets.

- Use the rule of three for your yes-set combinations.
- Move from the general to the specific.
- Start with externally verifiable truisms and lead on to internally verifiable ones.
- Pace then lead.
- Make suggestions ones that lead to relaxation.
- Keep related suggestions close together (relax eyelids, then cheeks).
- Connect sentences with *as, while, makes*.

Here is an example of a set of statements using this *interspersal* technique:

> *You have come here to relax; everyone relaxes in their own ways, as you begin to <u>get comfortable and ready to relax.</u>*
>
> *As you listen to my voice and feel the warmth of your hand on your knee, while the music plays you can relax the muscles around your eyes.*
>
> *They are becoming more and more relaxed, comfortably and completely and now it doesn't matter if <u>they stay closed</u>...*

You can continue in this way, embedding the relaxation suggestions within sets of truisms. At a suitable point you can insert an appropriate deepener.

You are now at the point at which everything is beginning to come together, all of the threads are intertwining, and you are about to make a leap in understanding. In the next do-it you will build an elegant induction and try it out. First of all you will start by writing down many scripts, yes sets, suggestions and inductions (we did) until they start to come naturally to you, and eventually, without knowing exactly how and when you internalised the skill, you will find yourself able to construct valuable, meaningful, eloquent and elegant inductions spontaneously. Do come on, let's start, do-it!

> **Interspersal: Do-It**
>
> Take the formula for the combination method given above, and using the yes sets that you have already created, the suggestions for progressive relaxation and the list of relaxing words that you have in your journal from the previous chapter, and build an induction using all of these elements.
>
> Try this out on a willing subject. Or record it on tape and try it out on yourself.
>
> Remember to use the simple content free suggestion for coming back refreshed and revived having worked on something of importance.
>
> You should write out at least 5 and more valuably 10 such scripts. Try them out, get feedback, and modify them, until you can create one spontaneously.

Before we finish with yes sets and move on to the next part of induction, here is something for you to think about; is a truism a truism when the answer is no?

> You wouldn't want to go into a trance before you are absolutely ready, would you?

GOING DOWN

We strongly believe that there is nothing that can't be achieved in light states of trance, and the value of deeper levels of trance is really in terms of convincers rather than the ability to do any particular work. Essentially it is easier to encourage the unconscious mind to make the right changes, when it is already convinced that it can do things that it never thought possible before (like induce analgesia, or allow one hand to rise involuntarily).

Many subjects don't realise that in light trance they have been hypnotized (and in many cases they won't have been, as most change can be equally well made in the waking state, or can happen before they go into trance) and for very good reasons, for some of them this means that the intervention won't work. We all, after all, now know about the power of suggestion. Mix this with the weight of expectation and you have an extremely forceful set of constraints.

At deeper levels of trance specific phenomena can be induced (catalepsy, time distortion) which can act as powerful convincers, but moreover people in deep levels of trance *FEEL as if* they are in trance. Apparently this is what trance is supposed to feel like!! There is one other factor; the deeper that the subject goes into trance, the more access the hypnotist has to the non-critical, subconscious mind. This means then that direct suggestions will have a more powerful effect. This is the basic technique used by traditional hypnotists (and especially stage hypnotists), so that suggestions (to improve, to stop smoking, to believe that a broom is Elvis Presley) are followed unquestionably. In fact, taking someone into a deeper level of trance makes the job of the hypnotist easier, even though in our opinion it is not strictly necessary.

We do recommend that you use at least one deepening technique in every formal induction, to act both as a convincer and to assist in your suggestions and interventions bypassing the critical mind. We have used variations of all of the following standard scripts with both individuals and groups. We merely list them here for you to include in your own scripts as you wish. You can see quite simply how they would work, and you may like to record them on a tape so that you can experience them yourself.

Simple counting

I will count DOWN from 3 to 1 and with each number you will double the relaxation..

3 ...double that relaxation, ..2 double it again...1... And double it again until you are so relaxed.

The staircase method

Imagine yourself at the top of a staircase, with 10 steps and a soft, comfortable bed at the bottom. With each step you take down towards that warm, comfortable, bed you become more and more relaxed, each step doubling your relaxation...and when you step off of that last step and into the bed you can fall comfortably into a deep and relaxing state of trance as you sink into the soft comfortable bed...(start counting) 10...9...down towards that comfortable bed... 8...(continue to intersperse suggestions for deepening trance) ......etc...1...that's right and as you step off into the bed you go ALL THE WAY DOWN..

The candle method

Visualise a candle, the wax dripping slowly down the side. Bit by bit the candle burns down more and more, the wax dripping, running ever so slowly down the side of the candle, eventually, effortlessly running into the pool of wax at the base of the candle. And the more the candle burns, the more the wax drips, the more the well fills with warm fluid wax, the deeper you go into trance

Doing it all together

As a sports coach or martial arts teacher, you will often find yourself working with groups rather than individuals: teams before a big game, students before a big grading or competition, or more likely a group of students, athletes, performers throughout their training from the moment they walk through the door on a Tuesday evening until the time they finally achieve their goals. Everything that you have learnt up to now, and everything that you will learn, applies equally well to groups or individuals. The inductions in this chapter, and the simple content free intervention, are designed to be used in any context, with any number of subjects, in hetero- or self- hypnosis.

Although the techniques are in general applicable to every situation, there are a few additionally things to consider when using hypnosis in a group situation. For the most part, they are common sense, but we'll list them here anyway.

The main thing that you must remember is that **everyone is different**. This means that you need to use an induction with truisms that apply to everyone in the entire group. The only way to do this is to pick universal experiences (discussed in the previous chapter). For example, if you ask a group to sit on the floor it would certainly be appropriate to *say "you are sitting there, listening to me, looking at me"* as long as they all were indeed looking at you. Some however may have their eyes closed. You can avoid problems by being less specific and more circumspect. *"You are sitting there, and I am speaking, you may be able to hear my voice, or you may be listening to something else. You are looking, somewhere..."*

The second thing to note is that **not everyone will go into trance at the same rate or to the same degree**. There are some ways of controlling this, for example by using a marker such as asking each member of the group to put their arm out and only to allow that arm to go down at the rate at which they go into trance. This then indicates who may or may not be responding to your suggestions. Once you learn to recognise the signs of trance which we have outlined earlier on in this book, you will be able to see who is responding and who is not, perhaps directing suggestions at individuals (not by name though, as each suggestion you make will be picked up by many people in the group), or by walking near them and talking directly to them.

The third thing to remember is that **trance is infectious**, just like yawning. As one person drops down into trance, so will the person on the left and right of them. If you begin by dropping into a trance, the group will follow. We have seen this in meditation session at the start or end of classes, in which we, or another teacher, enter a very peaceful, meditative state and very shortly afterwards, the rest of the class follows. So if you want the group to go into trance, then you follow this simple sequence: build rapport, pace, lead. They will follow.

> **Group induction: Do-It**
>
> Take one induction (and content free intervention) that you wrote in the last do-it, and, bearing in mind the three points above, re-write it to use with a group.
>
> Now try it on a group. Ask for feedback and build that into a re-worked script. Re-work it until it comes spontaneously.

AS I WAS SAYING

I continued speaking to my friend, who seemed to be listening very intently.

"Let me tell you how you can take someone deeper. It is a simple matter of counting down from three and with each count, doubling the relaxation. Three. Double it. Two. Double it again. One Double it one more time, allowing yourself to continue to float and drift ever downwards into trance. A healthy, relaxing, valuable, powerful trance that will enable you and allow you to start the process and make those changes that you wish to make, at a deep unconscious level. You have learnt an enormous amount today, just through listening to me. You have read and listened and thought and have begun to build a foundation of understandings and patternings that will allow you to take what you now know and build on it. Grow with it. Make it your own. And even as you sleep and dream, now or tonight, you can begin to sort through those learnings and absorb what is useful to you, retaining everything else because it will be useful to you at some point. And you can continue to do this, for as long as you need to. In order to consolidate your learning and begin to connect all of those strands, as they come together to form a whole. Now rest. And only when you are ready, come back to the here and now invigorated and refreshed, vibrant, ready and awake."

I waited for a while. It seemed very quiet. My friend seemed to be absorbed in something, perhaps he was thinking about what I had said, and the process that I had explained to him. I noticed that his eyes were slowly opening, blinking. He stretched, rolled his shoulders. Rubbed his eyes. Looked at me and smiled. "It's as simple as that," I said.

Chapter 7 – What's done is done

> *I shall be telling this with a sigh*
> *Somewhere ages and ages hence:*
> *Two roads diverged in a wood, and I -*
> *I took the one less travelled by,*
> *And that has made all the difference*
> *Robert Frost(1916),* <u>The Road not Taken</u>.

AND CAN'T BE UNDONE?

Milton Erickson (Rosen 1989) tells a story of a patient who, although always pleasant and bright, was living in a very different world. He was very quiet and would never really respond to any questions. One day, in an attempt to get through to this patient, Milton walked up to him, said hello, took off his own jacket then put it on backwards. He then took of the patient's jacket and put that back on him, backwards and said, "I'd like to have you tell me a story." The patient then began speaking.

We have already mentioned the importance of "going there first" way back in Chapter 1. The important thing to understand is that when working with a group or an individual, you will always have more success if you join them to some extent. At this point, if you have done all of the do-its and practised diligently then you should be able now to induce trance. And we have already given you some ideas of where to go when you have induced trance. In this chapter we look at some more advanced ideas, and will take things further. We will give you some more details about interventions and in particular discuss the value and use of visualisation, a technique that is well established in sports coaching as a method of psychological preparation (Liggett

(2002), Martens(1997)). But first, let's think a little bit about how we can use the idea of joining with the experiences of the client/athlete to begin to make changes and provide help without formally inducing trance. And here's the thing; you can only ever begin to work from where you are, you can never go backwards, only forwards.

GETTING TO KNOW YOU

One of the key skills required in life is the skill of rapport building. This skill is central to all social interactions, and is essential in counselling, coaching, teaching and hypnosis. And it is fundamental in negotiation and communication. Many people can automatically gain rapport, and there are always those whom you feel so comfortable with even after the first meeting. If you don't have rapport with your friends, family, partners or colleagues, you aren't going to get much done. If you don't have rapport as a coach, teacher or hypnotist you aren't going to be able to do good work.

Rapport is a relationship between two or more people. It is usually tacit, and spontaneously arises, but it can also be built. In some situations it may not come naturally, and so it must be constructed. There are a number of ways of doing this, enough ways to fill books (for example, Laborde (2001)) and bookshelves. But the principles are simple. There is actually only one principle and it is summed up in the following simple phrase - "You like people like you." Essentially this means that to build rapport, you have to match the other person as much as possible. Match their language, physiology, experiences and thought processes. In hypnosis it helps too to match breathing pattern (you can do this by watching their shoulders rise and fall).

Matching language and thought processes is essentially the same thing. From your understanding of modalities you should easily be able to see how what you hear can give you a feel for the way in which someone thinks. If they use mainly visual words, then they may be more visually oriented. The same goes for kinaesthetic and auditory. So to begin to build rapport, match their language, and so match their thoughts. Don't be blatant. If I say "you see what I mean," you can say "Well, that's an interesting perspective."

Building Rapport- Modalities: Do-It
Write a reply for each of these sentences that matches the modalities. For example:
Statement: *My view is that X is Y* – Reply: I see your point
You try:
I can't seem to focus in the problem *Something is stopping me moving on this* *I can't really tune into that idea* *That caught me off balance* *I have got a blank on that* *That doesn't really resonate*

You can match physiology simply by standing and moving and breathing in the same way as the person with whom you are trying to build rapport. But again not blatantly. If they have a tendency to move their right finger, you may choose to tap your foot in time with it. Sit forward and look interested if they are sitting forward and looking interested, sit back and relax if they are sitting back and relaxing. You will be amazed at how much more you can get done just using these simple techniques.

Grace Under Pressure

> **Building Rapport- Physiology: Do-It**
>
> Match someone. A great place to do this is in a queue or on a train or a bus. Pick someone and subtly begin to match parts of their physiology; the way they sit, the way they fidget and move. BE SUBTLE. Once you are sure you have built rapport then start changing your physiology a little (sit up, or slouch), you will be surprised at how they follow you (if you have matched appropriately that is).

Once you have built rapport by matching, you will find that as you move, the person with whom you have built rapport will move with you (rapport goes both ways you see). This is unconscious movement. You can then start leading. So if you want to help someone to go into a trance, first match them. Build rapport physically, and then as you see that they unconsciously match you, start going into a trance. They will follow. Next time you go into a shop or restaurant, match the person who serves you. Be enthusiastic if they are enthusiastic; be slow if they are slow. Smile. You'll be amazed at how accommodating they are, just because you have built rapport.

The easiest way to match someone is to match his or her experiences. You must have come across people who are interested in the same things as you are, with whom there is instant rapport. Not because you like the same things, but because you have experienced the same things. Walk into a room and say "isn't it cold outside." Notice that everyone will start nodding (as long as it is cold outside!!). You are immediately starting the process of building rapport.

As well as containing content that can be metaphorical and induce state change, stories are a wonderful way of sharing experiences and building rapport. If you are a parent, you are already a clandestine hypnotist. Do you read bedtime stories to your children? Do they begin to get sleepy the moment you start

"Once upon a time?" When I read to my children I slow my voice down, I use deep and relaxing tonality, I sit with them, leaning back, I breathe with them and I slowly relax as I tell them the story. Invariably they fall asleep, as I am reading, or barely last to the end. And I feel pretty sleepy too!!

Telling stories, then, is a great way of sharing experiences that are common to a group and building rapport. There are lots of stories in this book. They have a number of purposes.

The process of building rapport is simple but it does take practice. And remember - *be subtle*.

ALLOW ME TO INTERVENE

When you have a group or an individual in trance, the simplest way to utilise that trance state to good effect is, as has already been mentioned, to use content free interventions. The content is free, yet the process is not. In fact it is important to **be specific about the processes that are used to change and solve problems, and very unspecific about the content of the problem**. This is a general rule, and it will save you a lot of trouble and give you a lot of power to change.

The problem with content is that it will always mean something to someone. It is important in interventions to use ambiguity in your language so that individuals can make meanings relevant to themselves. In this way you don't have to know any detail about the other person or the specifics of their problems in order to help them make appropriate change. You never introduce inappropriate content and you allow the individual to be an active participant, as they have to fill in the content themselves.

As coaches and trainers you will have specific goals and states that you want to accomplish, and you will be able to find ways of doing this using content free interventions. Essentially this is as simple as saying, "Get motivated, do something, learn something and change now," but perhaps in a more subtle way, perhaps not. A completely content free intervention, might take the following form.

> *I would like your unconscious mind to select something of importance to you, something relevant to the problem, something that is meaningful and that brings to mind, your unconscious mind, one of many possibilities, ways of putting this problem behind you. Now take a moment of time, all the time you need, to evaluate this possibility and see if you feel that this is the most appropriate way. You might find that the first possibility is the best or you may find that there are others. Begin now, if you need to, to sort through your unconscious mind, find and evaluate as many possibilities as there are and choose one, one that will help you make the right changes right now.*

There is no content in the above script, just process. And the process is: **Find a number of possibilities, evaluate them and pick the best one. Then use that to change.** It is possible, and sometimes desirable to be more specific, especially in a sporting context. For example, if you wanted to relax someone you could say:

> *And go back through your memories to find a time when you were relaxed and peaceful. Calm and serene. Take all the time you need to find that perfectly <u>relaxing</u> time. <u>Relaxing</u>. And now as you come forwards to the here and now bring that <u>relaxing</u> with you.*

In this case, we are not giving any suggestions about what might be relaxing, we are just asking the subconscious to find a time that it thinks is relaxing and to recreate that feeling of relaxation right now. Notice that we <u>anchor</u> that feeling once established. Also notice that we are giving suggestions of relaxation, and that the words that we are using are associated with relaxation and calmness. The tonality of this, and every script, will continue to be important.

> **Content free script: Do-It**
>
> Now write a content free script for each of the following:
>
> motivation; energy; calmness; amusement.
>
> Can you write one that creates and anchors a combination of all of those?

Trust the unconscious, we do! Milton Erickson was famous for his exquisite use of language and his mastery of ambiguity. The unconscious mind is usually willing to try anything to help, and is a very powerful and valuable ally. Erickson would often just ask the unconscious mind to solve the problem, knowing full well that it could. The following simple script, informed by Erickson, can be of help in all areas of hypnosis.

> *Your unconscious mind knows what it has to do to improve your performance. It already has all of the resources and means at its disposal. If it is willing* (wait for response) *just take time now to allow it to go off and do whatever it needs to do to make those changes right now. It will let you know when those changes have been made and when you will see the benefits. Somehow.*

This neat intervention is misnamed, as it is completely free of any intervention by the hypnotist, and is entirely under the control of the subject. This is wonderfully effective in group situations where they are as many solutions to a problem as there are people in the group, and it is wonderfully effective in individuals. It is always better to find your own way. You learn more.

IMAGINE THIS

Some call it visualisation, for some it just feels right, others can hear the sounds they make as they perform perfectly. Visualisation is commonly used in sport as part of mental preparation. Most top athletes use visualisation in their training, and they use it for a number of purposes: to rehearse strategies and winning combinations, visualise best performance, imagine success, run through possible scenarios for the competition and build muscle memory. Chambers (1997) sees visualisation (sees....?) as integral to the mental preparation of an athlete, but Edgette and Rowan (2003) caution against too much reliance on visualisation.

Our view (there we go again) is that visualisation is one of a number of extremely effective methods of mental preparation and is always included, just because the visual system is one of the main representation modalities, in hypnotic intervention. Sports psychologists point to two types of visualisation, internal and external. *External visualisation* is a sophisticated feedback method, in which the athletes watch themselves or another athlete performing a given activity through the use of video. This is an excellent way to examine the exact movements of a technique, and to begin a modelling exercise. You will recognise this as a dissassociated method. It is also retrospective, looking back on past performance.

Internal visualisation can be both dissociated and associated, and importantly, it relates to future pacing. There are two ways of watching the film that you run in your mind; as if you are looking through your own eyes, or as if you are watching yourself. You can watch yourself performing an activity perfectly over and over again. It helps to draw connections between parts of the activity and build muscle memory subconsciously.

> **Building muscle memory: Do-It**
>
> Close your eyes, and imagine that you are watching yourself performing a specific technique or form (this is a particularly good way of learning the movements of a form, or kata, in order).
>
> Start at the very beginning of the movement and slowly move through to the end. Make the picture bright and bold and compelling. See yourself in the picture and now run the film, watching yourself.
>
> Now rewind. Run the film backwards. And now run the film forwards again. Every time you run the film, forwards and backwards, try to notice something different about your movement. Something key.
>
> Run the film as many times as you can, each time making the movement even more perfect and the film even faster. Now try the movement yourself. How does it feel?

Associated internal visualisation can help to build anchors and kinaesthetics associated with good performance. It is exactly this technique in which you can find, and benefit from, your very own Doris. The technique is the same, running a film of the perfect performance, but this time you are in it, seeing and feeling and hearing the performance as if you are doing it. As you run this performance through with you in it, know that the performance is perfect and notice how you feel, what you see and what you hear. When you do this technique or form for real, then you will know by what you see, feel and hear that you are performing perfectly.

Martens (1987) points to three key aims in visualisation in sports: Sensory awareness, vividness and control ability. *Sensory awareness* refers to the associated visualisation and the use of sub-modalities. *Vividness* is key in developing the finest granularity of experience; the more vivid, bright, compelling the images are the more distinct the experiences will be and the more accurately you will be able to anchor a perfect performance. *Control ability* is the ability to manipulate and control the images when desired to increase motivation and performance.

Visualisation works best when you are in a relaxed state, and guided relaxation in trance state is extremely effective. It can help to reduce both mental and physical signs of stress as well as being an effective preparation for an activity. The following is a group relaxation, based upon a visualisation technique, that I have used at the start and end of a class, and prior to competition to reduce stress and pre-competition nerves. You might like to try it out on yourself (perhaps you could record it and play it back whilst you relaxed?) and then on your students.

Seashore relaxation – Visualisation

And now I want you to make yourself comfortable in whichever way makes sense for you. You may like to sit, or lie or lean or whatever...That's right, you need to shuffle and get yourself comfortable, now. Now I would like you to close your eyes and begin to let your mind go, just for a little while. Go on a journey, a journey of relaxation. And I don't know just how relaxed you will become as I am talking, and I can only guess at how quickly you will become that relaxed. From the top of your head to the tip of your toes, right now, as you let go of all the tension, all the stress and all of the worry from every muscle and allow yourself to drift. Floating. Just as you might see a piece of seaweed floating on the water, at the seashore. Perhaps paddling your feet in the warm water, feeling your toes sinking ever so slightly into the sand as you watch the waves washing in and out...in and out, in and out, ever so slowly, ever so regularly and yet each one different. Each one curling and twisting in its own way, just as you relax in your own way. Waves of relaxation, waves of warm blue seawater, bringing, floating, drifting, and washing the flotsam and jetsam out to sea. And as you make your way back to the warm, golden sand of the beach, ready to drop on your towel , and relax even more deeply, your mind begins to wash away your cares and stresses and strains. With every step you take. Lying down on the towel, you notice your hand on the sand, the blue sky above and the clouds, wispy, floating across the sky. Lie there and take all the time you need, equal to one minute of clock time, to allow your subconscious mind to do whatever it needs so that you are able to re-access this feeling of calm and relaxation whenever you need to, and so that you will awaken renewed, invigorated, refreshed, calm and relaxed ...(pause)... That's right and now that you have made those changes you can begin the process of returning to the here and now bringing with you all of the resources that you need right now. In your own time open your eyes and come back...

This script takes just a few minutes to read through and yet can have a profoundly relaxing effect. A word of caution though, before any specific visualisation: please make sure that everyone in the group will find the context relaxing. Someone with a jellyfish phobia may not appreciate a trip to the seaside to paddle their toes!! It is always a good idea to check by asking. For example, I would ask..."Does everyone like to go to the seaside?" and then watch for responses. It is not enough just to take verbal responses at face value. Look for the signs that this may not be a pleasant experience for someone (you should already know how to do this by observing basic physiology).

Visualisation is a very powerful approach, and is much used in the sports coaching arena. However, as you now are very well aware, it is not the only method of mental preparation. It is one of many possibilities and can be combined with more direct methods, to form more and more effective interventions, both formal and informal.

Grace Under Pressure

And now, let's pull everything together. Let's see if we can join up the dots. I wonder what the picture will be?

Chapter 8 - Joining up the dots

> *No man can reveal to you aught but that which already lies half asleep in the dawning of your knowledge*
>
> *The teacher who walks in the shadow of the temple gives not of his wisdom, but rather of his faith and lovingness.*
>
> *If he is indeed wise he does not bid you enter the house of his wisdom, but rather leads you to the threshold of your own mind.*
>
> *The astronomer may speak to you of his knowledge of space but he cannot give you his understanding...*
>
> Kahlil Gibran, <u>The Prophet</u>.

UP TO THE THRESHOLD

You don't need this chapter. You may not be aware of it yet, but you already know everything that you need to know in order to improve yourself, your students, your team, and your athletes, even your friends and family. However just as the string becomes stronger when the strands are wound together, you will, by consolidation, by joining up the dots, give shape, form, and strength to your understandings and your ability to elegantly and efficiently use hypnotic language, ideas and principles in all aspects of your life.

You see, we have purposely stayed away from the idea of techniques. We don't subscribe to the idea that it is beneficial to learn anything by rote. We have provided frameworks, ideas, examples and all of the content you need to work at this level. Of course nothing beats experience or practical training, and there is always more to learn and directions in which to grow. We have only really introduced the basics of the use of hypnosis, but isn't that wonderful? It means that you don't know it all, and that there is much, much more to learn. You have just taken the first few steps on a very exciting journey, and if you have done as we have suggested and completed all of the do-its, you will be able to - Do-it, that is. And all of the people around you will benefit from your newfound skills and ability,

Still though, in order to add shape and form to your tacit learning, and perhaps to introduce some "aha" moments (you know, those moments when something suddenly jumps into your mind) we have chosen to use this chapter to recap, consolidate and outline. Read this chapter before you read the others, and it won't make sense, but come back to it again and again as you look for reminders, ideas, frameworks, and you will find it very valuable. You will enjoy this chapter, mainly because you'll be surprised about what it is that you already know. And at the end of it you get to give yourself a little present.

Excuse us for being formal

There are two ways to approach the use of your new skills in a sporting and martial arts context (in fact in any context), either formally or informally. *Formal methods* are those that are set up as hypnosis (and as a result set certain expectations) and follow through a relatively formal framework that usually will include a trance induction and defined intervention. Informal approaches are those which happen spontaneously, or if planned at all, without any specific indication of hypnosis, or without hypnosis at all.

Joining Up The Dots

Let us begin by summarising the things that you have learnt about in this book, some of them tacitly and some directly, in no particular order:

- Anchoring
- Representation Systems
- State
- Rapport
- Suggestions
- Goal setting
- Creating compelling desires
- Inductions
- Deepeners
- Interventions
- Tonality
- Pacing and Leading
- Storytelling

These are the elements that you can now put together in any number of ways to begin to form exquisite connections for motivating change and setting new directions. In a formal setting, in which you were trying to motivate a student or athlete you might put them together in a process such as this:

General Process for Hypnotic Work with Groups or Individuals

1. Build rapport through using representation systems, and perhaps storytelling.
2. Establish the key drivers and modalities for whatever state you wish to elicit
3. Start the induction.
4. Deepen trance.
5. Build a compelling goal or state. Use the drivers that you have established earlier on.
6. Anchor it.
7. Re-enforce with suggestions
8. Give time for the subconscious to integrate and work on new learnings
9. Emerge from trance

Of course, trance is not a prerequisite for effective intervention, although any single focus of attention that you might find when concentrating on anything, is trancelike. You are more likely to be in a more informal setting, before a big game, or in a class situation, and there won't be the chance for formal approaches or trance. It may even not be appropriate. Yet there is so much that you can do to change state (yours and others) through applying the simple ideas that you have learnt here.

Storytelling is a wonderful way to generate different states. Stories can be teaching tales, metaphors or just stories, and they can be exciting, motivating, calming or thought provoking. Storytelling builds rapport, engages people and breaks the ice. We are collectors of stories; you might like to start this hobby too. It will be a wonderful surprise when you find that within your collection you have just the story for just that time and place. Because stories can take time in the telling, and because you have both the conscious and unconscious attention of your listeners, suggestions can be fruitfully interspersed in them. In our more advanced book we will explore these ideas a little more deeply. But if you begin to collect, use and construct stories in different situations, you will discover all by yourself.

The other skills that you have learnt are important not only in your coaching, training and competing, but are also valuable to you in building relationships and setting and achieving goals. The use of good tonality, positive language and state management can mean the difference between degrees of success in all aspects of your life and the lives of those around you. Practicing these skills and using them formally and informally will change the way people see you and how you see them. You have worked hard to come this point and so now it is time to reward yourself.

DOING IT FOR YOURSELF

You have come a long way, and you have learnt an enormous amount about how to effectively use hypnosis in martial arts and sports for all sorts of powerful purposes. You have learnt to work with individuals and groups, and you now have all of the facility to work with yourself. Not just informally, using anchors or representation systems to generate and control feelings, but formally through self-hypnosis.

Self-hypnosis can be very useful for:

- General relaxation, and reducing stress and tension;
- Working on a problem with your subconscious;
- Installing specific behaviours or working on suggestions.

It is completely safe; during trance you are more aware of your surroundings than usual, and you will be able to arise from trance easily and quickly. We have already noted that trance is a naturally occurring phenomenon, and that there are some good examples of self-hypnosis, specifically in sports and martial arts. For example: being "in the zone"; when you have found your Doris; or during the performance of a form, technique; during a race or a game; in gradings, tests and demonstrations (especially breaking demonstrations!!).

Rather than just letting this occur naturally, you can channel the self-hypnosis process and use it to positively benefit yourself. One of the most common ways of inducing self-hypnosis in the martial arts specifically is through "focus" on the *tan tien* or *Hara*. Concentrating on that little spot three fingers above the naval, to the exclusion of everything else. The easiest way to induce self-hypnosis almost anywhere and any time is to use the progressive relaxation method on yourself. Simply relaxing from top to bottom, or bottom to top, then using one of the deepeners that you have already learnt.

It is important that you use self-hypnosis positively, and to this end you may want to write a specific suggestion to install once you are in trance. Of course, once you are in trance you are not really in a position to give yourself complicated suggestions, so a little trick is to write a suggestion on a piece of paper (taking care to formulate it appropriately) and decide on a single key word which you will associate with this suggestion. For example, you may choose to use self-hypnosis to stop you biting your nails, you could use the key word "Nails" to be associated with the suggestion "I have healthy and long nails and I cut them when they need to be shorter." Say the keyword, and then the suggestion over and over, maybe 20 times. When you are in trance, you only then need to say the keyword, and the associations will fire off[7].

When you are ready to come out of trance, just give yourself suggestions to awake, refreshed and revived. Allow yourself to come out at a comfortable rate, only as quickly as you are ready to. Don't rush. Note the time before you started, and the time you completed. You'll be surprised. You may have been in trance for no time at all, or for much longer than you thought you were.

Now its time to give yourself a present. We'll be here when you get back.

Self-Hypnosis: Do-it
Give yourself a present. Anything you want. Write a positive suggestion, go into trance and install it. Wake yourself up invigorated, refreshed. Enjoy.

---

[7] This excellent approach to self-hypnosis using trigger words to fire off suggestions, was shown to me by Richard Rizymski.

AND FINALLY...

So here we are, almost at the end. Or is it the beginning? More likely it is the end of the beginning. And where you go from here is entirely up to you. We have given you all you need to start using hypnosis exquisitely for yourself, your students and your families and friends. By all means try these ideas, the scripts and approaches, and as you find them more and more useful you may like to seek practical training. We would certainly recommend it, as however good you become, good quality training from professional practitioners is invaluable, just for the feedback and the practical advice. It will also give you confidence and the ability to deal with all sorts of situations. You may even want to take this knowledge further and pursue hypnotherapy as a career. Why not, you can do anything, can you not?

So let's see how much you have engaged in the process, how much you have learnt, how much you know. You will be surprised to find how easy this do-it is for you now, especially compared to how difficult it would have been if you had tried it before you read the book. But now you have.

Can you do it? Do-It
Here is your last do-it. If you have engaged in the processes of this book it should be simple. In a way it is a test (doesn't that word evoke some interesting states and memories), and it is a straightforward one.
Go through the book, chapter by chapter, picking out all of the places that you can find where we have used the techniques tools and ideas explored in this book. We don't mean in places that you expect to find them, we mean everywhere else. In the stories, in the text, in the dialogue. You will find metaphor, rapport, anchoring, ambiguity, content free interventions and more. If you know where to look that is.

Grace Under Pressure

But before you do go off to the Dojo or Gym, following your own path we have a few words of caution and advice for you.

Chapter 9 – There be dragons

> *"I understand you're the best golf instructor in the area?"*
> *"Well I don't know about that."*
> *"Can you teach me how to get out of sand traps?"*
> *"Sure...Follow me".*
> *The two men walked out of the golf shop and went to the driving range, ignoring the sand area all together.*
> *"Wait a minute; I thought you said you'd teach me how to get out of sand traps?"*
> *"First, let me teach you how not to get into them."*
> Paraphrased from <u>The Little Red Book</u> by Harvey Penick

DO THEY BREATHE FIRE?

These dragons that we speak of are not the ones St George had to slay but they are dragons nonetheless, and from your perspective, with your newfound knowledge, are very, very real. We have been where you are right now, the point at which the real learning begins, and we have learnt some tough lessons while we have been on the path. In this last chapter we want to share some of our experiences with you. Now of course, you are well aware of the power and purpose of stories, and we hope that you will both enjoy and learn from these, all of which are to various degrees amusing, some of which may be slightly sad, some embarrassing and some... well we will let you be the judge.

Grace Under Pressure

Sticks and stones will break my bones but names will never hurt you!

Ultimate fight

I first met my co-conspirator 20 years ago, and we were young dumb and full of many things, including lots of testosterone, which was flying around in our bodies. We were at a course and at the end paired up to do some light sparring, just as a warm down. The sparring started off gently enough but after a while things escalated. Neither of us was prepared to step back. Neither of us was prepared to examine the situation, we had an amazing amount of self-belief. Of course we began sparring harder and harder, as neither of us, from a martial art point of view, wanted to lose face. The punches, and in particular the kicks were getting progressively, harder, and neither of us was willing to show pain. We were in our own version of an ultimate fight! In many ways we were in a hypnotic trance, together, but we weren't able to recognise the benefits although we would feel the pain later. We both ended up very hurt, in more ways than one.

You see, belief is a powerful thing. One of our most influential teachers, Richard Bandler, refers to belief as *the express train of hypnosis*, and with all vehicles that are able to travel at high speed you have to know where and how to apply the brake. Newton's third law of motion which says that for every action there is an equal and opposite reaction, is relevant here. So if you don't know how to drive fast then please do stay in first gear until you can cope with second. There is plenty of time and with your growing skill and competence you will come to experience something neither of us knew or would accept 20 year ago.

Content free

One course I did with some new students focused on metaphors. It also looked at how martial arts could have a generative effect and help people make changes. Following my own advice, in the group inductions and relaxations I was very content free. Perhaps too content free? The script had a line that said something like *"you can choose to have the courage of your dreams and act them out."*

Later that night I was on a date with a new girlfriend. Of course I was anxious to impress her. While she was at my flat I received a telephone call from one of my students, who had been at the course earlier that evening. She professed her undying love for me, stated that I was the answer to her problems and explained that we should have children together.

Imagine then, that whilst trying to be empathetic and redirect and reframe, I am also trying not to let the gist of the conversation slip out to my very new girlfriend. She may have understood, but this was a very new relationship, and there wasn't much of an evening left.

In whatever capacity you work, especially in group-work, you will not know the complete history of those with whom you are working. The majority of people are well balanced, but you will come across people who have experienced or are experiencing periods of great stress; some even will have a mental health problem. Some may not know that they do. Some of this will be apparent to you and some of it won't. There *are* dragons out there. If you work with people then although you need to be *content free* you do need to know that the person that you are working with makes this *content specific*; in their own special way. And that content may not be as balanced as you may think.

You are never going to be a hundred percent sure that the interventions that you use aren't going to have some unbalancing effect for certain people with certain circumstances at certain times. But this is no different to any social interaction, in which you can say the wrong thing and spark an unwarranted reaction. You are much better placed, with your skills of sensory acuity, rapport and content free language, to avoid these problems or at least head them off. And you can pre-empt them to some extent by acting responsibly and asking your students in a non-intrusive and non-challenging way, questions that will allow you assess whether there is likelihood that they have an ongoing or previous mental health problems.

You can do this in a variety of ways. For example, we use a health questionnaire asking about general health (including mental health), and we may also ask for a doctor's letter. Most doctors will gladly respond to a request for an assessment of suitability for training. In the letter that you give to the students to take to their doctor, you should include information about the physical aspects of the training and also about the use of sports hypnosis in your classes and training. We always invite the student to a very informal interview to gauge their responses and to try to understand their history. None of this would prevent someone from training with us and benefiting from our Hypnotic techniques, but it does allow us to pay particular attention where we need to, and to modify and adapt our training programmes to individuals.

We are additionally fortunate to have a clinical psychologist as part of our training team and she is an invaluable source of advice. Of course we understand that this is not usual, but we do recommend that you make contact with your local health service clinical psychology department as a point of referral. Perhaps introduce yourself through a letter and then book an appointment to chat about your proposed work. We know that this sounds like a lot of effort, especially if you are only going to be using sports hypnosis sparingly in your training, but should you find yourself working with someone who does need professional help, you will know a psychologist who will be able to provide invaluable assistance.

Anger management

One night whilst teaching I was working with a student who asked if the relaxation techniques we taught could help with the management of anger. Of course they can, and I said so, but I wondered why this student had asked the question. You see they seemed to have a most lovely nature, and as far as I could tell wouldn't have said "boo" to a goose. She said that she was asking on behalf of their partner who had a problem with this part of their character. I asked if I could help, and she said that she would try to see if he would come along to the next session. Despite the clues, I still hadn't worked it out. It came to light later that this person was a serial abuser.

Because of your unique position as teacher, mentor and coach, for many people you may well be the first point of reference for some psychological input. We must stress however that sports hypnosis is not a substitute for professional therapy or counselling. We have honestly lost count now of the number of times that people have shuffled up to us at the end of a course or coaching session, waited until everyone had left and asked about help with a specific problem. We have professional training and are able to offer some degree of limited help. We are both qualified hypnotherapists, one of us is a trained teacher and the other a psychiatric nurse and state registered paramedic. However we cannot offer full medical and psychiatric help within a therapeutic environment, and we wouldn't. We only offer help that is within the boundaries of our expertise and experience. If we are in any doubt at all we will always refer people to those with the appropriate qualifications, experience and training. Because we know you will find yourself in this position, we urge you to make contact with a qualified psychologist so that you can recommend someone, and hand over a business card, or even make the initial appointment yourself.

Now this may seem a little serious, and we don't want to deter you from practicing your skills. We just want you to know your limits and be prepared. On the flip side, the best bit is that we can't tell you how many people have been enriched and empowered, have learnt new skills and have had had a fantastic time doing it, by using these methods. They are very much in the majority.

A challenge

One night, a good number of years ago, I was teaching a class in new dojo that we had recently started up. After a few weeks the class had built up and was quite large and successful. This particular night there were a few new faces (quite large and ugly faces they were too). These characters were from a local Karate class, a competitor it transpired, and they did their best to make a mockery out of all the techniques, in full view of the class. Of course they made themselves look foolish, but at the time I didn't see it like that. It eventually got to the point where I had had enough. I challenged them aggressively to leave or experience the effectiveness of the training themselves (not a very clever thing to do, but we grow, don't we?).

I accepted their offer to go outside, and the class followed us out. Sometimes belief can be a very powerful thing, and I certainly was confident in my techniques. I took the fight to them taking the first one to the ground, he made a lot of noise and the others backed down and off they went. I am embarrassed by this event now, you see, because, with the benefit of age and experience, I now know that I would react differently. I would apologise if necessary, step back, and have the maturity and sense to walk away. None of us really has anything to prove.

You should be aware that when you start to use the powerful techniques that you have learnt in this book, very occasionally you would find people whom are resistant. People who purposefully try to discredit and challenge you. These people seem to enjoy seeing you fail and being part of that. I remember well a time when we asked a group to shut their eyes and prepare for a relaxation session and two particular students forcibly kept their eyes open, coughed and laughed, trying all they could to disrupt the experience for those that wanted to be part of it.

What do you do in this situation and with these people? Well it is a unique opportunity for you to see how good you have become, but why bother? Once you recognise that you can take horses to water but sometimes they are not thirsty, then you recognise that the problem lies with them and not you. Take our advice, ask these people to leave.

CHEN AND YANG

Yang Lu Chan is the founder of the most famous and now most global form of Tai Chi, Yang Style. There are a number of versions of the story of how he came to acquire his skill but by far the one most often told is the following:

As a ten year old, Yang set out from his home in Hebei province to find work and to make his fortune. His path lead to the Chen Chia Kou village, home of the Chen family, famed as the possessors of secret martial techniques, and indomitable fighters. He secured work with the Chen family and showed himself to be honest and loyal. By chance, Yang discovered the Chen family members training in secret, and settled down to observe. He watched and listened from his hiding place in a tree, night after night, memorising techniques so that he could practise them later in private. It is told that this went on, year after year, for ten years.

One day, when the Chen family were out together, with Yang accompanying, Chen Chang Hsian (the head of the family) was challenged to a duel. At this time, fame could be won by challenging and defeating a well-known master, and Chen was well known. As was the custom at the time, senior students first took on the challengers on behalf of their teacher. They were all beaten. Then Yang stepped up and defeated them all, using the secret techniques of Chen Tai Chi. Of course Chen recognised the techniques and asked for an explanation, fearing that a member of his family had betrayed their secrets.

Yang explained how he had learnt, and Chen was impressed. He put Yang through a daily ritual of silent morning meetings, for a year. One day while Yang watched his teacher meditating, he thought he saw him lean forwards, and then suddenly found himself thrown across the room. Chen was still sitting in his seat. This was notification of Yang's acceptance into the clan. He trained for a further twenty years and was eventually told by Chen that he had become a master in his own right and should now continue on his path.

Yang became a famous fighter, known for his prowess with the spear, and eventually became the teacher of the Imperial guard. Even he though suffered tragedy when his granddaughter was killed whilst practising spear technique.

There Be Dragons

There are ways of learning, and sitting in a tree and observing is one of them. Make sure though that you watch carefully. Practicing what you have observed is also very important, and feedback is essential to make sure you are practising it correctly. Finding a good teacher, a mentor, and having him accept you, as a student is a sure way to improve your skill. Reading and learning and studying everything you can about other teachers, approaches, ideas, will improve your knowledge and broaden your abilities. A good teacher will support this. There comes a point when, to continue the process of becoming, you will want to make your own way, your own choices, develop your own style. This way you can contribute to a community of practice and give back to it.

Don't forget to get out of the tree and practise. And as soon as you feel ready, take the next step. And then the next, and the next. We look forward to reading *your* book!!

There was a certain man who was a master of the spear. When he was dying he called his last injunctions:

I have passed on to you all of the secret techniques of this school, there is nothing left to say. If you think of taking the discipline on yourself then you should practice diligently with the bamboo spear, all day. Superiority is not just a matter of technique.

Yamamoto Tsunetomo. <u>Hagakure</u>

Grace Under Pressure

Appendix – The wizards spell book

This appendix gives some sample scripts that can be used as the basis of development of your own scripts. Some include a simple induction and some suggestions/interventions, the later few assume that the client is already in a trance state and have less explanation. The aim is to provide templates that pull together a number of the threads and strands in the previous pages. We urge you not to read these scripts out verbatim. In fact this may not even be possible, as they are meant to be spoken, and as such make full advantage of the ambiguity of spoken English, so by applying strict grammatical rules to the transcripts and scripts we change their nature, this is why sentences seem to run on and you may not be sure where the breaks are supposed to be. We urge you then to take these scripts and modify them, then use them as if they were your own. Make them your own. Enjoy.

MOTIVATION

This is a script that you can use at the end of class or session. The words of the coach are given in italics. "Stage direction" is in plain text.

> *You have worked hard tonight. I have seen some big improvements and more importantly some very subtle improvements! Talking to you individually throughout the session has given me positive feedback that you are learning. And now you are tired, having had a successful session. I feel you can allow yourself to relax and feel good with the knowledge that you have worked for it.*

The Group are sitting down in semi circle.

So having made a successful start lets give you the mental edge as you are sitting here listening to the sound of my voice lets choose a quiet place where you would feel relaxed

The coach asks the group for examples of relaxing places. They may offer for example: the beach, the countryside, a park, their study, or even the bath

You guys and gals certainly know how to relax don't you?

The group smile and nod (but not all and the coach makes gentle eye contact with those not in agreement)

You must have somewhere you been or a time or a place where you have felt calm and confident?

The group reluctantly nod one still remains, others smile

That's right

Coach makes gentle eye contact and waits for positive resonance

There we go so we all have a place to go so lets take time now to go inside and really relax. Perhaps you can take a few breaths of air into your lungs now and as you breath in and out every breath can ease and relax you now that you are sitting here, you can take time now to change your position now or later, and if you hear someone move or gently realign themselves so that they are comfortable that's alright as it's all part and parcel of allowing themselves to enjoy and really experience the process of letting go, even of the tension in their bodies now that we are going to that special place you have already chosen. Perhaps you can feel sometimes they just don't have a place

At this point you should do a good head to toe relaxation (see earlier in the text, or use the relaxation script in this "wizards spell book").

Appendix

> *And you can feel the changing sensations as you relax while you can remember a time when you felt truly motivated*

Up until now your voice tonality has been gently downwardly inflected but the word motivation is now upward and vibrant, it should sound motivating.

> *That's right, seeing what you see hearing what you felt and feeling what you feel. Imagine you are back at the start of the lesson with those feelings now, that's right really feel motivated. How much faster, quicker, leaner are you going to be? Run through the lesson with every second just like a movie clip adding those feelings of motivation that's right and now when you have finished take those feeling and pop out into next week, allow yourself to feel motivated before you go for a run, gym session, hear your self and see yourself and feel you self really step into that picture now and seeing with your eyes as if you were there now, that's right and choose a word, any word - like motivation - and say it to yourself and every time you say it have those feelings and pictures and sounds radiate throughout your body and back into your body in a constant loop, that's right*

Watch the group now pace and lead pay attention to what each one is doing if you think one or two are not there gently repeat the process slowly

> *Now having worked hard and having enjoyed the session and put all the motivation you need to have into the future you can start to come back to the present, Now refreshed, alert and allowing your unconscious to integrate all of these learnings in a safe and appropriate manner for you. You can open your eyes now only as fast as you can have a small or large smile and grin motivated to enjoy life with a capital E.*

Tonality is very up-beat.

Critical Thinking:

To help guide you through this script, and consolidate your learning, here are a few questions. You should know the answers, and if you don't, then there is something that you didn't do. So go back and do it.

- ❏ Why should you ask the student's for input at the start of the script?
- ❏ How many representational systems were used at beginning and why?
- ❏ Why would you make reference to students making noise and moving position?

RELAXATION

This is a simple relaxation induction that can be used either on its own or as part of an induction. It is important to note that not all relaxation needs to learn to induction and intervention. Equally it is important to be aware that any relaxation does lead to an altered state, which can be utilised beneficially.

This script uses a general top down/ bottom up relaxation method, setting it up using yes sets at the start. Note also that it uses a reference experience but unlike the last script does not specify it. Notice also the subtle creation of a simple anchor.

> *And as you sit there, listening to the sound of my voice, breathing ever more slowly, aware of each and every breath, noticing perhaps the sensations of your body on the floor and certain other comfortable feelings beginning to emerge, a feeling of relaxation. I don't know whether it will start in the tips of your toes or at the top of your head, and whether then it will move up through your muscles or down through your muscles, relaxing each one of them bit by bit, little by little, until your body is completely relaxed. Take all the time you need to do that now. And as it does that you can feel every part of you sinking, floating, and drifting into a wonderful, relaxing state.*
>
> *As you relax your body bit by bit, you know that that is only half of the job, you need to relax your mind too. And as you realise this you can being to wonder, really wonder just how deeply you will experience the feelings of relaxation this time as being to you allow your mind also to go away to a*

comfortable, safe, relaxing place right now. Now I don't know where that is, and perhaps you have been there before. Perhaps this is the very first time, but you know just how calming and relaxing it can be. And as you imagine yourself there, see what you can see, feel what you can feel and hear what you can hear while you are there, immerse yourself in total relaxation in your relaxing place, relax your mind and relax your body. The more you relax one, the more you relax the other. And the further you go into your relaxing place. Take all the time you need to complete the relaxation to the depth and level of comfort that you want.

And you know that it is easy to relax. Any time you want to relax all you have to do is adjust yourself in to just the right position, and with your eyes closed, begin the process of going away to your relaxing place. Both mind and body.

Personal Power

What is personal power? Where does it come from? Why is it useful? These are all very valuable questions, especially since until we have defined what we mean by it, we can't really write a script to help create it.

When some people think and talk about personal power they seem to think that being powerful means being strong, winning, perhaps even fighting, being on top. This is certainly one approach. But when we think of personal power we think of having all of the resources at our disposal to enable us to what we want and to be who we want, with reference to the other people in the world. Accordingly this script allows you to create your own definition of personal power, and then build it.

Essentially the client is asked to find a number of resources that they would like to have that would make them feel personally powerful. Good examples are: confidence, motivation, organisation, stress-free, impartiality, inner-strength, good judgement. The presupposition is that at some point in time they have had some of each of these resources. In this script we take them back to re-access them, amplify them, and them bring them forward, stacked together, into the future and make them accessible through an anchor. Although we only access three states here, you can access, stack and amplify as many as are necessary. Five seems like a good number.

This script presupposes a trance state.

> *And now I want you to take some time to look at a number of situations in your future where you will need additional resources, where you can take the resources that you are already aware of and you know that just a little bit more of this one, or a lot more of that one, or this one that you didn't know you had yet, would be great, and would make all the difference, would give you that edge, would help you improve your time, your performance, your ability to cope even better. That's right. Now I want you to identify three resources that you really would like, or like more of, you can test that they are the right ones by imagining yourself in those situations as if you had those resources already and seeing how much better you do. Take all the time you need to come up with your list of three, and test them to make sure that they are THE most beneficial.*

Pause, and wait until everyone appears to have finished.

> *That's right. And now I have a surprise for you, because those resources that you didn't know you had yet, that's because you had them all the time, you just didn't know it until now. Because I want you to pick the first one off of your list and go into your past and pick a time when you had that resource, even just a little bit.*

Pause. If it seems that someone can't find the resource they need you can say.

> *And if you really can't find it, even the start of it, the seed of it, then you can still pretend that you have it. In fact you can steal it. Why not think of someone who you know has it, make a picture of them performing whilst using it, and step into that picture, and in to them, see what they see, hear what they hear and feel what they feel, fully experience the resource AS IF you had it. That's right.*

Appendix

And now go back to that time when you know you had the resource even just an little bit, or you can steal it, but make a picture of that time, see through your eyes, feel what you felt and hear what you heard, what were you saying to yourself? What could you say to yourself to make that resource even more powerful? That's right. Now amplify those feelings by changing the picture, maybe make it bigger, or smaller, or darker or lighter, or bolder or dimmer, or panoramic or bordered, whatever it takes to take that feeling and amplify it so that you no longer have just a little bit but now you have a whole lot, a massive amount of that resource, and call that resource X. Fully experience the state, allow it to grow and grow and build resource-X within you. That's right. Resource-X. And now put resource – X to one side, maybe by thinking of something else, anything else, I don't know what that will be as long as it is nondescript, it doesn't matter.

And now we do the same with two other resources, Resource-Y and Resource-Z, breaking state between each one. Use the script above.

And now we have those three resources X, Y and Z and we have amplified them and made them into the resources you need for the future, much more than they were but not as much as they can be. And we need to combine them, collapse them into a single resource that you can apply wherever and whenever you need this personal power.

So think of a time in the future when you are going to need these resources. Make a picture of that time, see yourself in the picture, and take that picture and push it out in front of you, exactly where it should be and just far enough so that you can put representations of resource X, resource Y and resource Z one behind the other, in front of it. And now what I want you to do is imagine you are on a rocket, and that that rocket is going to shoot you through Resource-X, Resource-Y and Resource-Z, collecting them on the way straight into the picture of that situation in which you need resources X,Y and Z. Into that situation where you have that personal power. But not yet. Because I want to you make sure that you have Resources –X and Y and Z as fully amplified as possible. And then when you have, get ready, because I want you to shoot through really fast and right into that situation and fully experience it with all of Resource-X and Resource-Y and Resource-Z at your disposal. With XYZ Personal power. Are you ready. Then Shoot.

Notice the physical reactions of the client (Group) you should be able to notice changes in them, if not, go back and do it again, and really make sure you amplify the responses.

And now from where you are, fully experiencing the benefits that having Resource-X and Resource-Y and Resource-Z all at once bring you, you can lay out all of those times in the future that you would benefit from having this degree of XYZ Personal Power, all of them, even those that you haven't even thought of yet. And now lay them out one behind the other just where they should be, and get back on your rocket and take XYZ Personal power with you and shoot all the way through as fast as you can. And when you have gone far enough, stop and turn round and see how far you have come. Now that's personal power.

And now float back to where you are now bringing XYZ personal power with you and also anything else you have learned from this experience. Now think about a time in the future that you know you are going to be able to access and use XYZ personal power. How does that feel? Do you see how far you can go? Do you feel how good you are going to feel? Do you hear the resounding sound of your success?

You can come back to the here and now in your own time, bringing with you all the learnings and understanding that you have now, and all of the valuable things that you have uncovered. And of course, XYZ personal power. All the way back with you and all the way onwards into your future.

Critical thinking

- Can you identify how anchoring was used in this script?
- Suggest a suitable tonality for various points in the script.
- If you knew the specific states that were being required by the client, how would you change this script?

ENERGY

What does it mean to have energy? For some, in simple terms this means being able to draw on that extra ounce, or find some hidden reserves. Some want to sleep less and train more, some just don't want to feel as tired. There are all sorts of things that can give us energy, specifically foods that are high in sugar or carbohydrate content, and we may be fooled in to thinking that Kendall mint cake or a mars-bar will do the trick. Then again stimulants such as caffeine can help us stay awake (but to what detriment to the body) and at the really low end of the scale, steroids are sometimes employed for strength, stamina, energy and all manner of other things. Clearly there is a physical dimension to energy, but there is also a mental dimension. Quite apart from the mind-body connection, getting in the right state can give you energy just when and where you need it. Motivation, for example is a great way to get energy, I always feel more energetic when I am motivated to do something. But why not go to the nub? You have them go back and experience a previously energetic state and anchor it. But that would be too simple (although it would work), especially for the last script in this book.

There is also the question of spiritual energy, and healing energy. Chi is often considered as a specific form of energy and meditation, chi gung and other forms of directed exercise are designed to build it. In this script we use this idea, the idea that you can generate energy internally, to build energetic behaviour and feelings up to such a level that the student is absolutely full of energy. Notice the use of a variety of representation systems, and of course, the ubiquitous anchor, we do want to be able to re-access this state when we want it.

This script can be used extremely well without introducing trance, and it is particularly effective during meditative or chi gung practice. However it works equally well in a trance-like state. The student and or client is asked to hold their hands in font of them or resting on their lap, as if holding a very lightly onto a large beach ball resting it on their forearms, in a relaxed way. It helps to visualise exactly this. This is essential because the sensations that occur when you hold your arms this way are the very sensations that we are going to take and grow into a full and energetic feeling.

> *And now relax your shoulders; they should be down, heavy, soft. Imagine that you have a beach ball resting lightly on your forearms, you can't drop it but you are not holding on to it, it is resting, lightly, pushing your elbows ever so slightly out, and extending your fingers. And as you rest there, listening to the sound of my voice, feeling your arm resting on your knee, you can begin to notice certain sensations, and I don't know if the sensations in your left hand or in your right hand are the more evident. It may be a warmth, it may be a tingling, it may be both, it may be a lightness, or a heaviness it might be all of these at once, or perhaps its something else.*

Take your time with this process, it does take a couple of minutes before the hands begin to tingle and generate warmth as the blood runs to them (on account of them being lower than the heart).

> *And allow that sensation to build, first in one hand and then in the other, and you may like to imagine that there is a small dot of white light just there, and that as the sensation grows so too does the light, and that as the light grows so too does the sensation. You can begin to move that light and the sensations with it, up one arm, along your chest and into the other arm, all the way to the fingers, where it joins the light and the sensations in the other hand. And it can jump across your fingers back into the first hand, twice as big, twice as powerful, and begin its journey again. And as you allow this ball of light to go round and round on its journey, from one hand, through your chest and into the other hand it becomes twice as big and twice as powerful with each rotation, faster and faster as it grows, your hands becoming warmer, tingling, your arms becoming warmer and tingling until it is a constant stream of energy rotating and growing, filling the space between your arms and becoming a big ball of light and energy sitting just like a beach ball, resting on your arms, growing. And you can feel its energy, and it is your energy.*

Appendix

And now take that ball of white light and push it in to your body at the centre and as you do allow that light to explode and separate inside your body, shooting out to every part of you, from the tip of your toes to the top of your head, filling every cell with energy as it expands from within, from the centre. Feel that feeling of being full of energy, and double it, double it again and again until you are so totally full of energy that you want to run and jump and shout and laugh, but not yet. And you are so full of energy. That's right.

This is your energy, you made it, and you can control it, and you can store it. Now in a moment I am going to ask you to pull that great ball of expanding light back into a ball the size of a tennis ball, and as you do you can leave each cell with as much energy as it needs, and maybe a bit more. Because you will never run out of energy, you know how to make more and you can allow your subconscious mind to replenish your energy store every night while you sleep, so that you always have more than enough each day. And when you have that ball of concentrated energy, take it and place it in your centre, where you know how to access it. Every night it replenishes and grows, every day you know its there and know how to access it, just by letting it explode in to every cell, that's right allow it to explode right now and fill every pore, every vessel, every muscle, every part of you. And enjoy it. And now bring it back to the centre.

And as you come back to the here and now, you can bring that energy with you, storing it in your centre, knowing how to replenish it and how to use it. And it feels good. Notice just how warm your body is now, notice that tingling and light feeling, you feel superhuman, you feel full of energy. Go for it.

Critical thinking

- What is the anchor? Is there only one?
- How many representation systems are in use?
- What changes would need to be made to this script to make it into a script suitable for physical regeneration and healing?

Appendix - Distinctions

SUBMODALITY DISTINCTIONS

The following list of submodality distinctions may assist you in fine tuning and coding internal representations. This is not a definitive list, we are sure that you can fins even more.

Visual	Auditory	Kinaesthetic
Moving/still	Volume	Temperature
Framed/ Panoramic	Tempo	Texture
Brightness	Tone	Vibration
Colour	Pitch	Duration
Distance	Richness	Movement
Contrast	Direction	Pressure
Movement	Location	Weight
Associated/Dissociated	Rhythm	Density
Size	Inflection	Location
Brightness	Spatial	Constant

CONSCIOUS - UNCONSCIOUS MINDS

These distinctions explore the difference between the conscious and unconscious minds.

Conscious	Unconscious
Logical	Creative
Deliberate	Automatic
Critical	Non-Critical
Concrete	Abstract
Discerning	Accepting
Guided	Autonomous
Constraining	Free
Limited	Unlimited

Bibliography

BandlerR. & Grinder, J. (1977) . <u>Frogs into Princes</u>. Real People Press.
Bandler, R (1982). <u>Using your Brain for a Change</u>. Real People Press.
Bandler,R & Grinder (1975). <u>Patterns of the Hypnotic Techniques of Milton H.Erickson, M.D. Volume 1.</u> Meta Publications.
Bateson, G (1972) . <u>Steps to an Ecology of Mind</u>. Ballentine Books. New York.
Caroll , L (1999). <u>Alice in Wonderland</u>. Walker Books.
Chambers, D (1997). <u>Coaching – The Art and the Science</u>. Key Porter Books LTD.
Drager, D. (1977). <u>Classical Bujitsu.</u> Weatherill inc. New York.
Edgette ,J. & Rowan, T.(2003). <u>Winning the Mind Game</u>. Crown House Publishing.
Freud, S (1915/1988). The Unconscious. <u>The Major Works of Sigmund Freud</u>. Encyclopaedia Britannica. William Benton.
Horwood, G (2002). <u>Tai Chi Chuan and the Code of Life</u>. Dragon Door.
Jarvis, M. (1999) <u>Sports Psychology</u>. Routledge.
Laborde, G (2001<u>). Influencing with Integrity</u>. Crown House Publishing.
Liggett, D (2000). <u>Sports Hypnosis</u>. Human Kinetics.
Harada, S (1998). <u>The Essence of Zen</u>. Kodansha International Ltd.
James, T (2001). <u>Hypnosis – Experiencing Deep Trance Phenomenon.</u> Crown House Publishing.
Martens, R (1987). <u>A Coaches Guide to Sport-Psychology.</u> Champaign.
McDermott, I and Jago W (2000). <u>The NLP Coach</u>. PiatKus Press.
McGill, Ormand (2003). <u>The Secrets of Dr Zomb</u>. Crown House Publishing.
Rogers, A (1998). <u>Teaching Adults.</u> Open University Press.
Rosen, S (1989). <u>My Voice Will Go With You: The teaching tales of Milton H.Erickson</u>. Norton.
Sieh,R (1992). <u>Tai Chi, The Internal Tradition</u>. North Atlantic Books.
Tsunetomo, Y (1983) <u>Hagakure.</u> Kodansha International Ltd.

Index

A

Aims · *70*
Amnesia · *58, 61*
Anaesthesia · *58, 59*
Analgesia · *58, 59*
Anchoring · *11, 22, 23, 24, 30, 33, 36, 54, 55, 78, 107, 109, 110, 117*
　Negative · *23*
Anger · *125*
Auditory · *34, 36, 50*
Automatic Processes · *62*

B

Bandler · *23, 32, 76, 87, 122*
Belief · *17, 26*
Black-belt · *9, 67, 68*
Breathing · *20, 37, 38, 40, 56, 62, 92, 102, 103*

C

Catalepsy · *54, 58, 59*
Coaching · *11, 74, 101, 102, 111, 116*
Combination method · *92, 94*
Communication · *18, 30, 102*
Compelling · *78*
Confidence · *27, 35, 69, 70, 74, 76, 119*
Confusion · *61*
Content free
　Script · *85*

D

Deepener
　Candle · *96*
　Staircase · *96*
Deepening
　Methods of · *88, 95, 96*
Defence · *43*
Dictionary · *31*
Dissociation · *60*
Distinctions · *32, 34, 35, 36, 41*
Doris · *53, 54, 58, 63, 109, 117*
Dragons · *121, 123*

E

Erickson
　Milton · *87, 101, 107*

F

Formal · *114*
Future Tense · *49*

G

Gibran, Kahil · 113
Goals · *68, 70, 71, 72, 73, 76, 77, 78, 106, 115, 116*
Grading · *39, 47, 67, 97*
Grinder · *23, 32, 87*
GroupWork · *123*
　Induction · *98*

H

Hallucination · *54*
   Negative · *57*
   Positive · *60*
Hara · See Tan Tien
Harmony · *36*
Hypnosis · *16, 107*
   Hetero · 82, 97
   Self · *82, 117, 118*
   Sports · *124*

I

Induction
   Formal · *86, 95*
   Interspersal · *94*
   Interspresal · 93
   Yes Set · *90*
Intervention
   Content Free · *106*
Interventions · *85, 95, 97, 101, 105, 106, 107, 108, 114, 124*

J

Journey · *20, 29, 56, 110*

K

Kata · *47,* 55, *57,* 109
Kick · *18, 20, 62, 64, 72*
Kickboxing · 24
Kinaesthetic · *34, 36, 50*
Kung Fu · *47*

L

Language · *46, 47, 49, 79, 88, 102, 105, 107, 113*
   Negative · *47*
   Positive · *47, 116*
Leadership · *21*
Lord of the Rings · *43*

M

Macchu Picchu · *29*
Matching · *103*
   Language · *103*
   Modalities · *103*
   Physiology · *104*
McKenna, Paul · *37*
Modalities · *32, 33, 34, 37, 38, 51, 103, 108, 115*
Motivation · *39, 45, 73, 107, 110, 133*
Muscle memory · *62, 64, 108, 109*
Mushasi · *9*

N

Negative · *58, 60*
Neural system · *62*

O

Outcome · *70, 71, 72, 73, 74, 76, 77, 78*
   Well Formed · *76*

P

Pavlov · *23*
Pep talk · *49*
Personal Power · *137*
Phobia · *23, 111*
Power · *22, 105*
Power Circle · 11, 23, 24, 25, 27, 36, *77*
Practice · *87, 105, 128, 129*
Preparation
   Mental · *111*
Progressive Relaxation · *83*
Psychologist · *124, 126*

R

Rapport · *30, 90, 92, 93, 98, 102, 103, 104, 105, 116, 124*
Relaxation · *82, 87, 88, 136*
  Sea Shore · *110*
Relaxing words · *45*
Representation systems · *33, 34, 50, 51, 52, 89, 115, 117*
Rhythm · *36*
Roger Bannister · *26*

S

Script · *50, 82, 84, 87, 91, 92, 107, 111, 123*
  Patter · 82
  Relaxation · *84*
Self Defence · *64*
Shakespeare · *43, 44, 52*
SMART · *72, 73, 74, 76, 78*
Soundtrack
  Submodalities · *37*
Sports psychology · *25*
Stories · *10, 18, 19, 21, 30, 101, 116*
Storytelling · *9, 105, 115, 116, 121*
Subconscious · *48, 49, 56, 61, 81, 82, 87, 95, 106, 111, 115, 117*
Submodalities · *32, 34, 35, 36, 38, 50, 51, 77*
Suggestions · *47, 48, 49, 58, 73, 79, 85, 93, 94, 96, 98, 106, 115, 116, 117*
  Direct · *48, 90, 95*
Sweet spot · *55*

T

Tai Chi · *127, 128*
Tan tien · *117*
Teaching · *20*

Time Distortion · *58, 59*
Trance · *55, 57, 58, 61, 63, 81, 85, 87, 94, 96, 97, 98, 99, 101, 104, 105*
  Bringing out of · *86*
  Deepening · *115*
  Indicator of · *56*
  Induction · *82, 83, 85*
  Levels of · *57*
  Naturally Occuring · *79*
  Phenomena · *57*
  Relaxation in · *110*
  Signs of · *54*
  States · *83*
Trance Phenomena · *95*
Truisms · *88*

U

Unconscious · *61, 62, 63, 87, 92, 99, 104, 106, 107, 116*
Utilising · *85*

V

Visual · *34, 36, 50*
Visualisation · *22, 25, 101, 108, 109, 110, 111*
Voice · *18, 19, 20, 21, 26, 88, 89, 91, 93, 97, 105*
  Nasal · *19*
  Tonality · *107*

W

Wilkinson, Johnny · *53, 54, 63*

Y

Yes Sets · *89, 91*

SEMILLION

HYPNOTHERAPY AND SPORTS HYPNOSIS TRAINING

Train with the authors.

A combination of distance learning and practical workshops

- Flexible learning to suit your lifestyle and budget.
- Hypnotherapy Diploma ratified by the United Fellowship of Hypnotherapists

Courses:

- Hypnotherapy Diploma
- Certificate in Sports Hypnosis
- Certificate in Permissive Hypnotherapy
- One day, Introductory Hypnosis courses

We also work with private clients.

Details available on the semillion website
http://www.semillion.co.uk or by calling 01737 210818

Black Belt Hypnosis

www.blackbelthypnosis.co.uk

A course designed by martial artists for martial artists.

A one-day accelerated course, tailored to martial arts practitioners, instructors, coaches and competitors. As a martial artist you are already aware of the power of the mind, why not go that extra mile and turn your mind from a tool to an effective weapon or personal achievement?

Learn:

How to develop personal power

The keys to successful skill building

How to develop that mental edge

How to improve your physical performance, mentally

How to generate more motivation, more energy, more confidence

How to win, achieve, be successful

Do you want to get your black belt? Motivate yourself and your students? Make your team into a winning team? Improve your skill?

Then *this course is for you.*

Contact us at the web address above or call 01737 210818. for the next course dates.

This is a semiliion course.

Grace Under Pressure